I0438745

Knowledge and Understanding of Dissolved Solids in the Rio Grande–San Acacia, New Mexico, to Fort Quitman, Texas, and Plan for Future Studies and Monitoring

By Douglas L. Moyer, Scott K. Anderholm, James F. Hogan, Fred M. Phillips, Barry J. Hibbs, James C. Witcher, Anne Marie Matherne, and Sarah E. Falk

Prepared in cooperation with the U.S. Army Corps of Engineers, New Mexico Interstate Stream Commission, and New Mexico Environment Department

Open-File Report 2013–1190

U.S. Department of the Interior
U.S. Geological Survey

U.S. Department of the Interior
SALLY JEWELL, Secretary

U.S. Geological Survey
Suzette M. Kimball, Acting Director

U.S. Geological Survey, Reston, Virginia: 2013

For more information on the USGS—the Federal source for science about the Earth, its natural and living resources, natural hazards, and the environment, visit http://www.usgs.gov or call 1–888–ASK–USGS.

For an overview of USGS information products, including maps, imagery, and publications, visit http://www.usgs.gov/pubprod

To order this and other USGS information products, visit http://store.usgs.gov

Suggested citation:
Moyer, D.L., Anderholm, S.K., Hogan, J.F., Phillips, F.M., Hibbs, B.J., Witcher, J.C., Matherne, A.M., and Falk, S.E., 2013, Knowledge and understanding of dissolved solids in the Rio Grande—San Acacia, New Mexico, to Fort Quitman, Texas, and plan for future studies and monitoring: U.S. Geological Survey Open-File Report 2013–1190, 55 p., http://pubs.usgs.gov/of/2013/1190/.

Contents

Figures

Tables

Conversion Factors

Inch/Pound to SI

Multiply	By	To obtain
Length		
inch (in.)	2.54	centimeter (cm)
inch (in.)	25.4	millimeter (mm)
foot (ft)	0.3048	meter (m)
mile (mi)	1.609	kilometer (km)
Area		
acre	4,047	square meter (m^2)
acre	0.004047	square kilometer (km^2)
Volume		
cubic foot (ft^3)	0.02832	cubic meter (m^3)
acre-foot (acre-ft)	1,233	cubic meter (m^3)
Flow rate		
acre-foot per day (acre-ft/d)	0.01427	cubic meter per second (m^3/s)
cubic foot per second (ft^3/s)	0.02832	cubic meter per second (m^3/s)
Mass		
ton, short (2,000 lb)	0.9072	megagram (Mg)
ton, long (2,240 lb)	1.016	megagram (Mg)
ton per day (ton/d)	0.9072	metric ton per day
ton per day (ton/d)	0.9072	megagram per day (Mg/d)

Temperature in degrees Celsius (°C) may be converted to degrees Fahrenheit (°F) as follows:

°F=(1.8×°C)+32

Temperature in degrees Fahrenheit (°F) may be converted to degrees Celsius (°C) as follows:

°C=(°F-32)/1.8

Vertical coordinate information is referenced to the North American Vertical Datum of 1988 (NAVD 88).

Horizontal coordinate information is referenced to the North American Datum of 1983 (NAD 83)

Altitude, as used in this report, refers to distance above the vertical datum.

Specific conductance is given in microsiemens per centimeter at 25 degrees Celsius (µS/cm at 25 °C).

Concentrations of chemical constituents in water are given either in milligrams per liter (mg/L) or micrograms per liter (µg/L).

Knowledge and Understanding of Dissolved Solids in the Rio Grande–San Acacia, New Mexico, to Fort Quitman, Texas, and Plan for Future Studies and Monitoring

By Douglas L. Moyer,[1] Scott K. Anderholm,[1] James F. Hogan,[2] Fred M. Phillips,[3] Barry J. Hibbs,[4] James C. Witcher,[5] Anne Marie Matherne,[1] and Sarah E. Falk[1]

Executive Summary

Both quantity and quality of water in the Rio Grande have long been a primary concern for water-resource managers. The transport and delivery of water in the basin has been engineered, using reservoirs, irrigation canals and drains, and transmountain-water diversions to ensure an adequate water supply to meet the agricultural, residential, and industrial demand. In contrast, despite the widespread recognition of critical water-quality problems, there have been minimal management efforts to improve water quality in the Rio Grande. Of greatest concern is salinization (concentration of dissolved solids approaching 1,000 milligrams per liter [mg/L]), a water-quality problem that has been recognized and researched for more than 100 years because of the potential to limit both agricultural and municipal use.

In order to address the issue of salinization, water-resource managers need to (1) have a clear conceptual understanding of the sources of salinity and the factors that control storage and transport, (2) identify critical knowledge gaps in this conceptual understanding, and (3) develop a research plan to address these gaps and develop a salinity management program. As a result, the U.S. Geological Survey, in cooperation with the U.S. Army Corps of Engineers, New Mexico Interstate Stream Commission, and New Mexico Environment Department undertook this effort to summarize the current state of knowledge regarding the transport of dissolved solids in the Rio Grande between San Acacia, New Mexico, and Fort Quitman, Texas. This effort specifically focused on the following three questions:

1. What is the spatial and temporal variability present in the concentrations and loads of dissolved solids in the Rio Grande?

2. What is the source-specific budget for the mass of dissolved solids transported along the Rio Grande?

3. Where do new dissolved solids enter the Rio Grande?

Dissolved-solids concentration data provide a good indicator of the general quality of surface water and provide information on the factors governing salinization within the Rio Grande study area. The pattern in dissolved-solids concentrations along the Rio Grande is one of increasing concentration with increasing distance downstream from Elephant Butte and Caballo Reservoirs. The concentration of dissolved solids in the Rio Grande doubles (approximately 500 to 1,000 mg/L) from below Elephant Butte Reservoir to El Paso and increases by more than a factor of 5 (approximately 500 to 3,200 mg/L) from below Elephant Butte Reservoir to Fort Quitman. Studies that have focused on dissolved solids in the Rio Grande study area can be categorized into three major groups, which are: (1) identifying the sources of dissolved solids; (2) characterizing surface-water processes that control the transport of dissolved solids, and (3) defining the role that groundwater processes play in controlling transport of dissolved solids.

Sources of dissolved solids have been investigated using three methods (1) synoptic sampling to identify locations where concentration increases, (2) spatial and temporal patterns within dissolved-solids loads, and (3) source determination through isotopic fingerprinting studies. During the past century, studies have investigated the hydrology/hydrogeology and associated water-quality conditions along the Rio Grande and underlying alluvial basins from San Acacia to Fort Quitman. During these investigations, researchers have identified areas of surface water and(or) groundwater that contain unusually high concentrations of

[1] U.S. Geological Survey

[2] Department of Hydrology and Water Resources, University of Arizona; New Mexico Environment Department (current affiliation)

[3] Department of Earth and Environmental Science, New Mexico Institute of Mining and Technology

[4] Department of Geological Sciences, California State University

[5] Witcher and Associates

dissolved solids or associated water-quality constituents. These areas have the potential to contribute significant amounts of dissolved solids to the Rio Grande and need to be considered for future investigations and(or) future locations of dissolved-solids mitigation efforts. Marked increases in the concentration of dissolved solids commonly coincide with contributions from agricultural drains, wastewater-treatment plants, regional groundwater, and upward-flowing saline groundwater. The locations of these areas containing elevated dissolved-solids concentration have been provided for the Socorro, San Marcial, Engle, Palomas, Mesilla, and Hueco Basins and include the (1) northern end of the Socorro Basins; (2) area surrounding Truth or Consequences, New Mexico; (3) southern end of the Palomas Basin through the northern end of the Mesilla Basin; (4) eastern and southern portions of the Mesilla Basin; and (5) area southeast of the El Paso-Hudspeth County line near Fabens.

The greatest factor, from the surface-water system, in controlling dissolved solids in the Rio Grande is the amount of water that is being transported or stored. Annual mean streamflow in the Rio Grande decreased on average by 840 cubic feet per second during 1934 and 1963, between San Marcial and Fort Quitman. Annual variation in streamflow is influenced primarily by climate (precipitation and evaporation) and management of Elephant Butte and Caballo Reservoirs (water storage and release cycles). Seasonal variation in streamflow within the Rio Grande study area is most evident at monitoring stations below Elephant Butte Reservoir. Streamflow conditions in this section of the river are categorized generally as irrigation (March–September) and nonirrigation (October–February) seasons.

Streamflow in the Rio Grande is highest during the irrigation season and lowest during the nonirrigation season. As a result, dissolved-solids concentrations vary from season to season with the concentration of dissolved solids in the Rio Grande between Caballo Dam and El Paso commonly twice as high during the nonirrigation season as compared with concentrations during irrigation season. Dissolved-solids loads during the irrigation season decrease by approximately 1,000 tons per day in the Rio Grande between Leasburg and Fort Quitman. These decreases in load are attributed primarily to irrigation diversions and losses to the underlying alluvial aquifer. Conversely, dissolved-solids loads during the nonirrigation season increase by nearly 900 tons per day between Caballo Dam and Fort Quitman. These increases in load are attributed to the inflow of dissolved solids from agricultural drains, wastewater-treatment plants, and groundwater with elevated concentrations of dissolved solids.

Seasonal variability in dissolved-solids loads also provides information on the critical role that the shallow groundwater system plays in the transport of dissolved solids in the Rio Grande in the study area. During the irrigation season dissolved-solids loads generally decrease between Leasburg and Fort Quitman primarily as a result of water being diverted from the Rio Grande to meet agricultural water-supply needs. Much of the dissolved-solids load carried by the diverted water infiltrates the shallow alluvial aquifer and subsequently is intercepted by agricultural drains and returned to the Rio Grande. However, in areas of extensive groundwater pumping, these dissolved solids are drawn deeper into the alluvial aquifer system and threaten the quality of the groundwater resource. During the nonirrigation season, dissolved-solids loads increase between Leasburg and Fort Quitman because of inflow from saline groundwater (Leasburg to El Paso) and freshwater dissolution of evaporite beds (El Paso to Fort Quitman). It is essential for water-resource managers to understand how groundwater transport processes collectively govern the transport of dissolved solids in the Rio Grande and how these processes influence the potential for salinity-mitigation efforts.

Many studies have mass-balance budgets that account for the mass of dissolved solids transported along the Rio Grande. Two types of budgets for dissolved-solids transport in the Rio Grande have been developed since the early 1900s. Basic budgets define the relation between the mass of dissolved solids transported by the Rio Grande into a specified reach to the mass of dissolved solids transported out of the specified reach. Complex budgets attempt to account for all sources (such as tributaries, agricultural drains, municipal wastewater effluent, mineral dissolution, and groundwater discharge) and sinks (e.g. irrigation canals, groundwater recharge, and mineral precipitation) of dissolved solids, such that mass balance between the inflows to and outflows from a specified reach of the Rio Grande equals zero. Results from the two types of budgets developed for dissolved solids indicate that (1) the inflow of saline groundwater, inflow of regional groundwater, and chemical reactions between mineral phases are the primary sources controlling dissolved solids in the Rio Grande, and (2) groundwater pumping and mineral precipitation are causing a net storage of dissolved solids in the Leasburg to El Paso and El Paso to Fort Quitman reaches of the Rio Grande.

Historical dissolved-solids data in the Rio Grande study area provide good information for determining the associated spatial and temporal variations and defining preliminary budgets; however, these data also facilitate the determination of data and knowledge gaps. Primary data gaps are the lack of coupled long-term streamflow and water-quality monitoring in the Rio Grande and major agricultural drains and limited groundwater seepage data (groundwater and surface-water interactions) outside of the Mesilla Basin. The initiation and continuation of these monitoring data are essential for (1) improving the current understanding of dissolved-solids transport in the Rio Grande study area; (2) establishing water-quality goals; (3) building tools/models for water-resource managers to more effectively manage water-quality conditions; and (4) assessing changes in water-quality conditions in the Rio Grande resulting from salinity mitigation efforts. Critical knowledge gaps exist in (1) understanding the hydrologic controls that govern the transport of elevated dissolved solids from known groundwater sources to the Rio Grande and how these controls influence the potential for interception or other mitigation efforts and (2) understanding the linkage between the surface-water, irrigation, and groundwater in the shallow alluvial aquifer systems and how changes in water-management and(or) climate may influence the quality of groundwater and surface water in the Rio Grande study area.

Looking forward, multiple water-resource managers from state and local agencies in New Mexico and Texas as well as many federal agencies have united to form the Rio Grande Salinity Management Coalition. The unifying goal for the Coalition is to reduce the amount of dissolved solids that are transported and stored in the Rio Grande study area; thus, ensuring that the Rio Grande water resources are of the quality that promotes the integrity and vitality of the agricultural, municipal, and ecological communities. The recommendations for additional monitoring for focused hydrogeology studies of the source of inflowing groundwater with elevated concentrations of dissolved-solids and model development for dissolved-solids transport will assist the Coalition in planning for, implementing, and evaluating mitigation efforts for dissolved solids in the Rio Grande. These recommendations are as follows:

- Monitoring:

  - Couple water-quality and streamflow monitoring in the Rio Grande and agricultural drains; undertaking this effort will further improve the current understanding of dissolved-solids transport and allow for (1) establishment of water-quality goals, (2) improved quantification of dissolved-solids loads, and (3) determination of long-term trends of dissolved-solids concentrations and dissolved-solids loads.

  - Perform groundwater-seepage investigations in the Rio Grande and major agricultural drains; the result of this effort will be the ability to quantify the flux of dissolved solids being delivered to and from the underlying alluvial aquifer.

  - Monitor groundwater water-quality conditions in the Mesilla and Hueco Basins; supporting this effort will allow for (1) quantification of current water-quality conditions, (2) evaluation of temporal and spatial changes in water-quality conditions, and (3) the potential to forecast future water-quality conditions based on changes in municipal and agricultural water demands within the Mesilla and Hueco Basins.

- Focused Hydrogeology Studies at Inflow Sources:

  - Map dissolved-solids concentrations in the Rio Grande and underlying alluvial aquifer using technology such as helicopter electromagnetic resistivity data; undertaking this effort will provide high-resolution 3-dimensional maps defining the spatial extent of areas containing unusually high concentrations of dissolved solids.

  - Perform hydrogeologic characterization of subsurface areas containing unusually high concentrations of dissolved solids; undertaking this type of study will provide critical information regarding subsurface-flow paths and the underlying geology that governs the movement of dissolved solids. Additionally, this type of study will provide information on how the underlying geologic structure and flow paths may influence the potential to intercept and mitigate the inflowing saline groundwater.

- Modeling of Dissolved Solids:

  - Develop models to simulate the transport and storage of dissolved solids in both surface-water and groundwater systems; undertaking this effort will provide models to evaluate the impacts that surface-water management, groundwater pumping, and climate variability have on dissolved-solids transport in the Rio Grande and underlying alluvial basins. Additionally, information provided by these newly developed models and the data-collection effort listed above will be used to refine the current mass-balance budgets for dissolved-solids transport in the Rio Grande.

Introduction

Availability of water in the Rio Grande Basin has long been a primary concern for water-resource managers. The transport and delivery of water in the basin has been engineered using reservoirs, irrigation canals and drains, and transmountain-water diversions to meet agricultural, residential, and industrial water-supply needs. Annual delivery of water to surrounding agricultural, residential, and industrial users is critical to ensure the associated social and economic vitality of these communities (Jackson and others, 2001). The quantity and quality of the water supply are factors that often limit the ability of water-resource managers to meet the ever-growing water-supply requirements.

The quantity of surface water available to meet various water-supply demands is influenced by many factors, including climate, population growth, and agricultural cropping patterns. Runoff from annual snow accumulation and summer monsoons serves as the primary source of water in the Rio Grande Basin; however, during extended periods of drought, runoff usually is inadequate to fully meet allocated water-supply needs (Booker and others, 2005). Added pressure to the quantity of surface water available for water supply is applied through population growth in Albuquerque, Las Cruces, El Paso, and Ciudad Juarez, as well as the replacement of agricultural crops, such as chilies, with crops that have greater water requirements, such as pecans. Nearly all of the water transported down the Rio Grande from the headwaters in Colorado is evaporated, consumed by the various water-supply demands, or lost to the underlying alluvial aquifer by the time the river reaches Fort Quitman, Texas (Rister and others, 2011). The combined effect of dry climate, population growth, and changes in agricultural cropping pattern causes the surrounding surface-water-users to become increasingly dependent on groundwater to meet the growing water demand.

Water quality also is a primary factor that can limit the availability of water for use within the Rio Grande Basin. The concentration of dissolved solids is a common measurement variable used to assess the general quality of water in riverine systems and provides a measure for the amount of dissolved-organic and inorganic compounds that are present in the water column. The majority of the dissolved-solids concentration in riverine systems consists of major ions, such as bicarbonate, calcium, chloride, magnesium, potassium, silica, sodium, and sulfate (Hem, 1992; Anning and others, 2007). These major ions occur naturally and are essential for plant and animal growth (Anning and others, 2007). However, elevated dissolved-solids concentrations may be detrimental to plant and animal species within an aquatic ecosystem and can result in reduced productivity of agricultural crops and increased costs for municipal and residential water treatment and use (Anning and others, 2007).

Concentrations of dissolved solids in riverine systems increase through concentrative or additive processes. Concentrative processes remove water from a riverine system but leave behind dissolved solids, which results in an increased concentration. Evaporation and transpiration are concentrative processes that increase dissolved-solids concentrations. Additive processes transport additional dissolved solids into a riverine system and can be categorized into three groups: (1) cyclical and surficial salts, (2) inflow of saline groundwater, and (3) anthropogenic salt inputs (Phillips and others, 2003; Anning and others, 2007; Hogan and others, 2007). Cyclical and surficial salts are delivered to riverine systems through atmospheric precipitation (rainfall and snowfall) and subsequent dissolution of salts accumulated on the land surface and in the soil. Saline groundwater contains elevated concentrations of dissolved-solids that originate from geothermal or nongeothermal sources. Saline groundwater can be derived from the dissolution of evaporite deposits, such as ancestral playa beds (Hibbs and Merino, 2007) and gypsum and calcite (Witcher and others, 2004; Bastien, 2009), sedimentary brines of connate or diagenetic origin (Phillips and others, 2003; Witcher and others, 2004; Hogan and others, 2007), or geothermal processes (Bothern, 2003; Witcher and others, 2004). Anthropogenic salt inputs are derived from a number of sources in agricultural, residential, and industrial areas of the basin. Examples of anthropogenic sources include fertilizers, residential water softeners, road salt, and industrial processes. These salts are often delivered to riverine systems through industrial water treatment, municipal wastewater treatment, or surface runoff.

The concentration of dissolved solids in the Rio Grande increases by nearly two orders of magnitude as water is transported from the headwaters in Colorado to Fort Quitman, Texas (Moore and Anderholm, 2002; Phillips and others, 2003). During the past century, dissolved solids in the Rio Grande Basin have been intensively studied. Early studies focused on identifying the spatial and temporal variability present in dissolved-solids concentrations and whether these concentrations would limit the supply of water to developing agricultural communities (Stabler, 1911; National Resources Committee, 1938). Studies also focused on quantifying the mass of dissolved solids transported from one reach of the Rio Grande to the next to determine whether salts were accumulating in agricultural soils (Wilcox, 1957; Wilcox, 1968; Williams, 2001). A major focus for studies during the past two decades is identifying factors that contribute to the increase in dissolved-solids concentration and loads measured along the Rio Grande (Moore and Anderholm, 2002; Mills, 2003; Phillips and others, 2003; Witcher and others, 2004; Hibbs and Merino, 2007; Moore and others, 2008). Researchers have been able to identify the dominant sources of added salts into the Rio Grande using a variety of hydrogeological, geophysical, and hydrochemical analyses. These sources include saline groundwater, wastewater-treatment plants, and mineral dissolution in the alluvial aquifer.

In order to address the issue of salinization, water-resource managers need to (1) have a clear conceptual understanding of the sources of salinity and the factors that control storage and transport, (2) identify critical knowledge gaps in this conceptual understanding, and (3) develop a research plan to address these gaps and develop a salinity management program. In 2009, the U.S. Geological Survey (USGS) in cooperation with the U.S. Army Corps of Engineers (USACE), New Mexico Interstate Stream Commission (NMISC), and New Mexico Environment Department (NMED) initiated a project to summarize the current state of knowledge regarding the transport of dissolved solids in the Rio Grande between San Acacia, New Mexico, and Fort Quitman, Texas (fig. 1). Sources of dissolved solids in the portion of the watershed located in Mexico were not assessed. The primary objective is to provide hydrologic information pertaining to three questions:

1. What is the spatial and temporal variability present in the concentrations and loads of dissolved solids in the Rio Grande?

2. What is the source-specific budget for the mass of dissolved solids transported along the Rio Grande?

3. Where do additional dissolved solids enter the Rio Grande?

In addition to addressing these three questions, secondary objectives were to provide information regarding gaps in the current state of knowledge and suggestions for future studies and monitoring data.

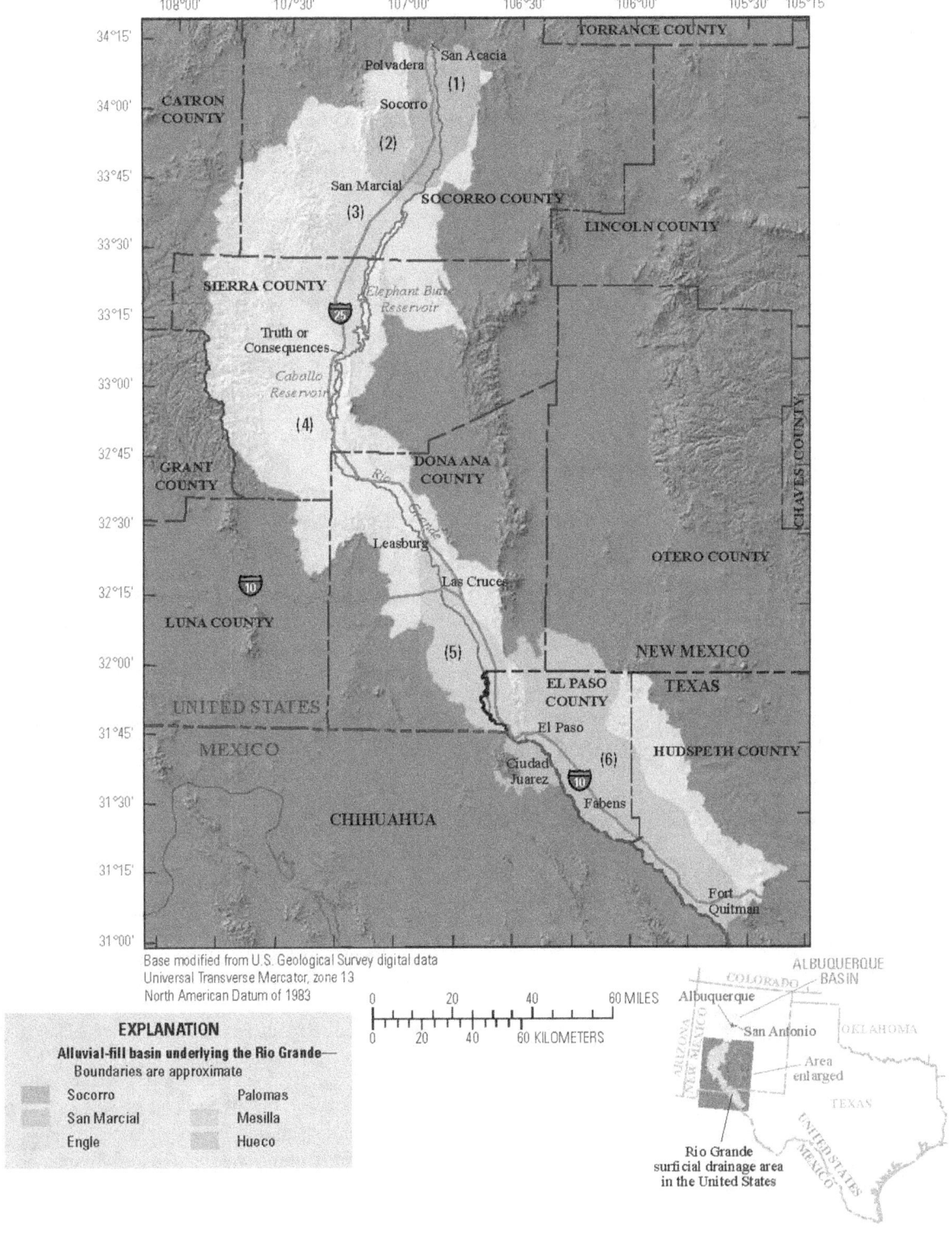

Figure 1. Map showing the Rio Grande study area (white area) and the distribution of the six alluvial-fill basins underlying the Rio Grande: (1) Socorro, (2) San Marcial, (3) Engle, (4) Palomas, (5) Mesilla, and (6) Hueco Basins. Boundaries of the six alluvial-fill basins are approximated from Wilkins (1986).

Purpose and Scope

This report addresses the current state of knowledge regarding the transport of dissolved solids in the Rio Grande and associated alluvial-fill basins between San Acacia, New Mexico, and Fort Quitman, Texas. This current state of knowledge is a synthesis of existing studies that addressed various aspects of the transport of dissolved solids in the Rio Grande study area. This report includes discussions of (1) spatial and temporal variability associated with streamflow, dissolved-solids concentration, and dissolved solids load in the Rio Grande, (2) dissolved-solids budgets for six reaches along the Rio Grande study area, and (3) the locations of groundwater and surface-water containing high concentrations of dissolved solids. Also included is a plan of study with recommendations for future studies and monitoring data that will result in a better understanding of the transport of dissolved solids in the Rio Grande.

Description of the Rio Grande Study Area

The Rio Grande is the fourth longest river system in the United States and extends from the southern part of Colorado to the Gulf of Mexico. The portion of the Rio Grande that will be discussed in this report extends from San Acacia, New Mexico, to Fort Quitman, Texas (fig. 1). Climate, surface-water flows, geology, water use, and water management all play important roles in the transport of water and solutes through the Rio Grande study area. Many of the studies that addressed the sources of dissolved solids in the Rio Grande study area have determined that the geology and hydrology of the underlying alluvial aquifers and the structure and management of the surface-water system have the greatest influence on dissolved-solids concentration in the Rio Grande (Phillips and others, 2003; Hogan and others, 2007; Moore and others, 2008). This section provides a brief overview of each of these physical features and the role they play in influencing the hydrology and water quality of the Rio Grande.

Climate

The climate of the Rio Grande study area and areas of the Rio Grande Basin that extend north of San Acacia, New Mexico, influences the hydrology and associated water quality through precipitation and evaporation. The average total annual precipitation that is delivered to the Rio Grande Basin is highly variable. In the northern mountainous areas of the Rio Grande Basin, average annual precipitation exceeds 50 inches, whereas average annual precipitation delivered to the Rio Grande study area typically is less than 10 inches (Ellis and others, 1993). The concentration of dissolved solids in precipitation and associated runoff and infiltration typically are low and considered a minor contributor of dissolved solids in the Rio Grande Basin. Dissolved-solids concentrations in precipitation range from less than 0.5 to 3.0 milligrams per liter (mg/L) (Anning and others, 2007).

Most precipitation delivered to the Rio Grande Basin is lost to the atmosphere through evaporation and transpiration. Phillips and others (2003) determined that approximately 75 percent of the water in the Rio Grande at the Colorado-New Mexico border is lost to the atmosphere through evaporation and transpiration by the time the river reaches El Paso, Texas. Evaporation and transpiration produce an approximate fourfold increase in concentration of dissolved solids in the Rio Grande between the headwaters in Colorado and Fort Quitman, Texas (Phillips and others, 2003; Hibbs and Merino, 2007; Hogan and others, 2007).

Streamflow in the Rio Grande Study Area

Streamflow in the Rio Grande study area decreases as water flows from San Acacia, New Mexico, to Fort Quitman, Texas, and exhibits considerable variability from year to year. The decrease in streamflow is a result of water withdrawals and streamflow losses, which exceed inflows (Wilcox, 1957). The majority of water in the Rio Grande as it enters the study area originates from mountainous regions of southern Colorado and northern New Mexico. Elevated streamflow conditions as a result of snowmelt runoff typically occur from May to August. Local runoff associated with summer monsoon rainfall also contributes water to the Rio Grande in the study area. Rainfall runoff from the mountainous regions in the Rio Grande study area is transported through a network of ephemeral channels; however, many of these ephemeral channels have flood-control dams that slow runoff, thus promoting increased seepage and evaporation. Groundwater discharge from the alluvial aquifers located within the Rio Grande study area also contributes to streamflow in the Rio Grande study area (Ellis and others, 1993). Additional contributions to streamflow occur through discharge from agricultural drains and municipal wastewater-treatment plants. Despite these contributions, streamflow decreases along the continuum of the Rio Grande study area because of losses through evaporation and transpiration (Phillips and others, 2003), irrigation diversions (Wilcox, 1957), losses to the underlying alluvial aquifer (Wilson and others, 1981), and surface-water and groundwater withdrawals for municipal water supply (West, 1995; Hibbs and others, 2003; Witcher and others, 2004; Eastoe and others, 2007).

The majority of the water in the Rio Grande that enters the study area is stored in Elephant Butte and Caballo Reservoirs (fig. 1). Elephant Butte and Caballo Reservoirs were constructed at the beginning of the 20th century as part of the Bureau of Reclamation's Rio Grande Project (Autobee, 1994). The primary purpose of these reservoirs is to store and release water for irrigation of agricultural crops in the Palomas, Mesilla, and Hueco Basins. Water is not released from these two reservoirs from October through February; consequently, flow in the Rio Grande below Caballo Reservoir during this period is small and water in the Rio Grande is derived primarily from groundwater discharge, agricultural drains, and municipal wastewater-treatment plants. Water is released from these reservoirs during March through September to supply water to irrigation districts throughout the study area. An additional part of the Bureau of Reclamation's Rio Grande Project was to construct a network of diversion dams and unlined irrigation canals to deliver Rio Grande water to irrigate agricultural crops (Autobee, 1994). Diversion dams route water from the Rio Grande to the irrigation canals, which route water to the agricultural fields. Approximately half of the surface water diverted for irrigation is transpired by vegetation or evaporated, whereas the remaining half infiltrates to the subsurface either through canal seepage or on-farm return flow to the alluvial aquifer system (Anderholm, 2002; Bastien, 2009). Shortly after the completion of the Rio Grande Project surface-water distribution system, groundwater levels rose and resulted in saturated and salt-enriched soils. A network of agricultural drains was constructed during the 1920s and 1930s to mitigate this problem. The purpose of the agricultural drains is to maintain the elevation of the groundwater table several feet below the surface of the fields by intercepting and draining shallow groundwater. Water in the agricultural drains typically returns directly to the Rio Grande.

The concentration of dissolved solids in the agricultural drains is typically 2 to 5 times greater than the concentration of dissolved solids in the irrigation canals and Rio Grande (Anderholm, 2002; Bastien, 2009). The increased concentration of dissolved solids in the drains has been linked to (1) evaporation and transpiration within the agricultural

fields (Hibbs and Boghici, 1999; Phillips and others, 2003; Bastien, 2009), (2) mineral dissolution (Witcher and others, 2004; Bastien, 2009), and (3) inflow of sedimentary brine groundwater (Moore and others, 2008). Thus, the irrigation canal and agricultural-drain network integrates processes that exchange high-volume, low dissolved-solids-concentration Rio Grande water with low-volume, high-dissolved-solids-concentration groundwater.

Alluvial-Fill Basins

The Rio Grande in New Mexico and west Texas flows through a series of alluvial-fill basins in the Rio Grande Rift. The Rio Grande Rift extends from southern Colorado through central New Mexico to near El Paso, Texas, and was formed approximately 30 million years ago as part of the widespread extension of the western United States (Keller and Baldridge, 1999). The Rio Grande Rift is described as a series of north-south trending downdropped basins (grabens and half grabens) that are connected end to end (Thorn and others, 1993). These basins are bordered on the east and west sides by areas of uplift, which commonly consist of Precambrian crystalline or Paleozoic sedimentary bedrock (Phillips and others, 2003). These series of connected basins are filled with alluvial and lacustrine sediment and range in depths from 13,000 feet (ft) to less than 100 ft (Wilson and others, 1981; Anderholm, 2002; Phillips and others, 2003). The north-south boundaries between each of the alluvial-fill basins are formed by convergence of the eastern and western structural boundaries or regional uplift, which brings the underlying bedrock close to the surface (fig. 2; Thorn and others, 1993). Bryan (1938, p. 198) simply describes the relation between the Rio Grande

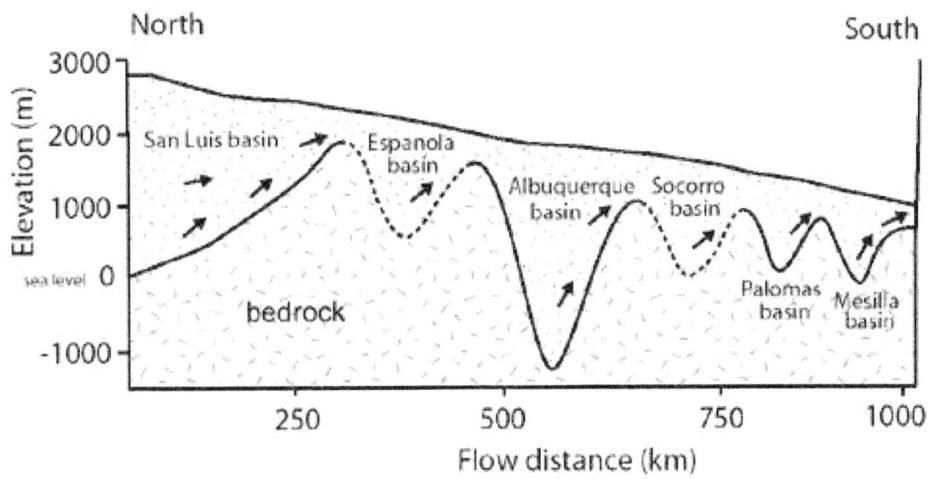

Figure 2.   Schematic hydrogeologic cross section of the Rio Grande Rift, parallel to the path of the river (from Phillips and others, 2003; used with permission).

and underlying alluvial-fill basins as "a stream flowing from one sand-filled tub to another through narrow troughs." Six alluvial-fill basins within the Rio Grande study area directly underlie the Rio Grande – the Socorro, San Marcial, Engle, Palomas, Mesilla, and Hueco Basins (fig. 1; Wilkins, 1998). Detailed descriptions of the geologic structure of the alluvial-fill basins can be found in Chapin (1971), Hawley (1978), Riecker (1979), Hawley and Kennedy (2004), Hawley and others (2005), and Hutchinson (2006).

Recharge to the alluvial-fill basins occurs as a combination of (1) mountain-front recharge, (2) inflow from adjacent aquifers, (3) infiltration of water from the Rio Grande, and (4) infiltration of irrigation water applied to agricultural areas (Ellis and others, 1993; Anning and others, 2007). Mountain-front recharge commonly is considered to be the primary mechanism for natural groundwater recharge in the alluvial-fill basins (Frenzel and others, 1992; Heywood and Yager, 2003; Anning and others, 2007). Mountain-front recharge is the infiltration of runoff from near basin margins (Frenzel and others, 1992; Heywood and Yager, 2003). This runoff originates in the uplifted and mountainous regions of the alluvial-fill basins and is subsequently transported through ephemeral channels. These ephemeral channels consist of porous substrate that facilitates the infiltration of runoff. In addition, most major ephemeral channels in the study area have flood-control dams, which further promote the infiltration of storm runoff. However, recent studies have found that a significant portion of the water that recharges alluvial-fill basins originates from the Rio Grande and irrigation network (Sanford and others, 2004; Witcher and others, 2004; Eastoe and others, 2007). The general flow paths that the regional groundwater follows in the alluvial-fill basins extend from basin margins toward the Rio Grande and southward from one alluvial-fill basin to the next (Ellis and others, 1993). The travel time for regional groundwater in the alluvial aquifer to move from groundwater recharge areas to groundwater discharge is on the order of 10,000 years (Anderholm and Heywood, 2003; Eastoe and others, 2007). Saline groundwater originates from geothermal or nongeothermal sources separate from the regional groundwater system, likely from a groundwater flow system in the bedrock underlying the basin, and seeps upward and mixes with the regional groundwater in the alluvial aquifer (Mills, 2003, Hogan and others, 2007, Moore and others, 2008).

Discharge from the alluvial-fill basins occurs through (1) direct discharge to the surface-water system, (2) evapotranspiration, (3) flow to adjacent alluvial aquifers, and (4) groundwater pumpage (Ellis and others, 1993). Direct discharge to the surface-water system occurs directly to the Rio Grande and through interception by agricultural drains. Groundwater discharge to the surface-water system is most pronounced at the distal end of each alluvial-fill basin (Wilson and others, 1981; Ellis and others, 1993; Phillips and others, 2003; Hogan and others, 2007). This discharge occurs because of the decreased cross-sectional area of the alluvial-fill basin resulting from the convergence of the eastern and western

structural boundaries (Ellis and others, 1993). The direct discharge of groundwater to the surface-water system has been identified as a significant mechanism for increasing the concentration and mass of dissolved solids in the Rio Grande (Wilson and others, 1981; Anderholm, 2002; Phillips and others, 2003; Witcher and others, 2004; Hibbs and Merino, 2007; Hogan and others, 2007; Moore and others, 2008).

During predevelopment times, the amount of recharge that occurred in the alluvial-fill basins approximately equaled the amount of discharge. However, the development of groundwater resources in each of the alluvial-fill basins during the past half century to meet municipal and agricultural water-supply needs has shifted the groundwater balance such that discharge exceeds recharge (Ellis and others, 1993; Anning and others, 2007). Groundwater is used to meet the municipal water-supply needs for the cities of Las Cruces, Santa Teresa, El Paso, and Ciudad Juarez, as well as to supply irrigation water and supplement surface-water irrigation supplies during periods of drought. The primary impacts of groundwater pumpage are localized reduction in groundwater levels and the reversal of groundwater-flow paths, from flow paths that historically flowed southward along the Rio Grande to flow paths that now carry water perpendicularly away from the Rio Grande (Wilson and others, 1981; West, 1995; Hibbs and others, 2003; Witcher and others, 2004). A secondary impact of groundwater pumping is the reduction of groundwater discharge to drains, which is especially evident during periods of drought.

Water Use

The majority of water use in the Rio Grande study area is attributed to three general categories – agricultural, municipal, and reservoir evaporation. These three categories account for greater than 95 percent of the water used in five counties within the Rio Grande study area – Socorro, Sierra, and Dona Ana Counties in New Mexico (Longworth and others, 2008), and El Paso and Hudspeth Counties in Texas (Texas Water Development Board, 2007). Of these three water uses, water supplied for irrigating agricultural crops accounts for 93, 30, and 89 percent of the total water used in Socorro, Sierra, and Dona Ana Counties in New Mexico, respectively (Longworth and others, 2008), and 50 and 99 percent of the total water used in El Paso and Hudspeth Counties in Texas, respectively (Texas Water Development Board, 2007). The Rio Grande is the primary source of irrigation water in the study area; however, groundwater often is used during periods of drought to ensure that the irrigation requirement for the various agricultural crops is met (Frenzel and others, 1992; Ellis and others, 1993).

The main population centers in the Rio Grande study area are Socorro (population 9,100), Las Cruces (population 75,000), El Paso (600,000), and Ciudad Juarez (1,300,000). Groundwater is the primary source of drinking water for the residents of these population centers. Municipal water supply accounts for 1.7, 1.5, and 7.7 percent of the total water used in Socorro, Sierra, and Dona Ana Counties in New Mexico, respectively (Longworth and others, 2008), and 45, and 0.3 percent of the total water used in El Paso and Hudspeth Counties in Texas, respectively (Texas Water Development Board, 2007). However, El Paso now uses both groundwater and Rio Grande water for municipal water supply (Hibbs and others, 2003).

The loss of water through evaporation from reservoirs accounts for 4 percent of the total water used in Socorro County and 67 percent of the total water used in Sierra County. The two primary reservoirs within these two counties are Elephant Butte and Caballo Reservoirs. In 2005, the total amount of water evaporated from Elephant Butte and Caballo Reservoirs was estimated to be nearly 102,000 acre-ft (Longworth and others, 2008). For comparison, the total amount of water consumed by the residents of El Paso in 2005 was estimated to be 136,000 acre-ft (Texas Water Development Board, 2007). Regardless of whether Rio Grande water is lost through evaporation from Elephant Butte or Caballo Reservoirs or from agricultural fields, the effect is a relative increase in the concentration of dissolved solids.

Factors Affecting Dissolved Solids

Several processes influence the concentration and load of dissolved solids in the Rio Grande in the study area. Concentration is a measurement that describes the amount of dissolved solids that are present in a specified volume of water. The units for the concentration of dissolved solids are commonly milligrams per liter (mg/L). However, the concentration of dissolved solids does not provide information on the quantity of dissolved solids that are being transported along the continuum of the Rio Grande study area. Load is a measurement that describes the mass of dissolved solids that are mobilized per unit of time. Examples of the units that are used to define the load of dissolved solids are kilograms per day (kg/d) and tons per day (tons/d). Information on the loads of dissolved solids is essential for the development of mass-balance budgets. The processes that influence dissolved solids in the Rio Grande study area can be grouped into three categories – those that alter concentration only, those that influence concentration and load, and those that influence only load.

Concentration

The loss of water from the Rio Grande through evaporation, agricultural transpiration, and riparian transpiration are dominant processes that affect only the concentration of dissolved solids in the Rio Grande. The concentration of dissolved solids is increased as a result of evaporation and transpiration; however, the increase in concentration is proportional to the loss of water such that the dissolved-solids load remains nearly constant (Moore and Anderholm, 2002; Anning and others, 2006). Many studies have investigated the extent that evaporation and transpiration have on the pattern of increasing dissolved-solids concentration along the length of the Rio Grande study area. These investigations used hydrogen and oxygen isotopes to estimate the total water lost through evaporation and to indirectly quantify the water lost through transpiration and found that the loss of water through these processes governs the increase in dissolved-solids concentration observed along the length of the Rio Grande study area (Phillips and others, 2003; Hogan and others, 2007; Eastoe and others, 2007; Moore and others, 2008). However, the increase in dissolved-solids concentration along the Rio Grande is too large to be produced through evaporation and transpiration alone (Phillips and others, 2003; Hogan and others, 2007).

Concentration and Load

Several processes affect dissolved solids in the Rio Grande study area by increasing both the concentration and load. These processes include (1) groundwater discharge, (2) tributary inflow, (3) industrial and municipal discharges, and (4) mineral dissolution, all of which involve the transport of additional dissolved solids into the Rio Grande. Several studies, using the ratio between chloride and bromide, have found that evaporation and transpiration alone cannot account for all of the increase in the concentration of dissolved solids observed along the length of the Rio Grande study area and that new sources of dissolved solids are needed to obtain the observed increase in both concentration and load (Phillips and others, 2003; Hibbs and Merino, 2007; Hogan and others, 2007; Eastoe and others, 2007; Moore and others, 2008). Studies also have employed various geochemical and isotopic analyses to characterize and identify the multiple sources and processes that add dissolved solids to the Rio Grande. Results from these studies indicate that the dominant processes that increase dissolved solids in the Rio Grande are the discharge of saline groundwater (Anderholm, 2002; Mills, 2003, Phillips and others, 2003; Witcher and others, 2004; Hogan and others, 2007; Moore and others, 2008) and mineral dissolution (Anderholm, 2002; Hibbs and Merino, 2007; Bastien, 2009).

Load

Dissolved-solids loads in the Rio Grande can be increased and decreased without changing associated dissolved-solids concentrations. Processes that decrease the dissolved-solids load without changing the concentration are those that remove water and associated water-quality constituents in equal proportions. These processes include (1) irrigation diversions, (2) municipal and industrial diversions, and (3) groundwater recharge. Processes that increase the dissolved-solids load without changing the dissolved-solids concentration are those that transport water having the same concentration of dissolved solids as the Rio Grande to the Rio Grande. Potential processes include the discharge of water from tributaries, agricultural drains, and industrial or municipal effluent.

Spatial and Temporal Variability in Dissolved-Solids Transport

Dissolved solids in the Rio Grande are influenced by many factors such as climate, water-management operations, groundwater and surface-water interactions, and various contributing sources. In order to better manage dissolved solids in the Rio Grande, water-resource managers need to understand the extent of the spatial and temporal variability present in dissolved-solids conditions and the associated processes that govern transport and storage. In the following sections, the spatial and temporal variability associated with dissolved solids in the Rio Grande are described. Understanding the spatial variability associated with dissolved solids along the Rio Grande will allow managers and researchers to determine the sources of dissolved solids and where these dissolved solids are entering the Rio Grande. Understanding the temporal variability exhibited in dissolved solids provides information on the effect that factors, such as climate and water-management operations, have on the dissolved solids over extended time periods along the Rio Grande. Data collected by Wilcox (1968) from 1934 to 1963 at Rio Grande at San Marcial, New Mexico (San Marcial); Rio Grande below Elephant Butte Dam, New Mexico (Elephant Butte); Rio Grande below Caballo Dam, New Mexico (Caballo); Rio Grande above Leasburg Dam, New Mexico (Leasburg); Rio Grande at El Paso (Courchesne Bridge), Texas (El Paso); and Rio Grande at Fort Quitman, Texas (Fort Quitman), were the primary sources of data used to evaluate spatial and temporal variability in dissolved solids along the Rio Grande study area.

Streamflow

Variability in streamflow is a primary factor that affects dissolved-solids transport in the Rio Grande study area. The concentration of dissolved solids is affected by streamflow through dilution or evaporation, or as the contributions from other sources and flow paths vary as a result of changes in water-resource management practices. Additionally, dissolved-solids loads are a function of streamflow and vary as streamflow changes from year to year and season to season. Therefore, it is important to first examine the spatial and temporal patterns in streamflow in order to determine how these variations influence the resulting patterns in dissolved-solids concentrations and loads. Streamflow data and associated statistics are specific to the 1934 to 1963 time period; however, the temporal and spatial patterns observed in

streamflow during the 1934 to 1963 period are related to more current data when applicable.

Spatial Variability in Streamflow

Annual streamflow in the Rio Grande study area indicates that streamflow decreased on average by 840 cubic feet per second (ft^3/s) between San Marcial and Fort Quitman during the 1934 to 1963 period (fig. 3). Annual mean streamflow measured in the Rio Grande at San Marcial was 1,041 ft^3/s. Management of Elephant Butte and Caballo Reservoirs and numerous irrigation canals and drains control streamflow in the Rio Grande between Leasburg and Fort Quitman (Moore and Anderholm, 2002). The effect of flow control by Elephant Butte and Caballo Reservoirs can be seen in the reduced variability in annual streamflow conditions for all stations below San Marcial (fig. 3). Annual mean streamflow measured in the Rio Grande at Leasburg between 1934 and 1963 was 901 ft^3/s. Approximately 300 ft^3/s was lost annually from the Rio Grande between Leasburg and El Paso (fig. 3). The depletion of streamflow from this reach of the Rio Grande was caused primarily by agricultural transpiration depletions of the surface water applied for irrigation (Phillips and others, 2003). Additional depletion of streamflow can be attributed to losses through municipal groundwater pumping at the Las Cruces and Cañutillo (located about 15 miles upstream from El Paso) well fields (Wilson and others, 1981), agricultural groundwater pumping (Wilcox, 1968; Wilson and others, 1981), and loss of water from the Rio Grande to the alluvial aquifer through seepage (Wilson and others, 1981; Newton and others, 2002). Mean annual streamflow measured in the Rio Grande at El Paso was 597 ft^3/s (fig. 3). An additional 400 ft^3/s, on average, was lost each year from the Rio Grande between El Paso and Fort Quitman. Much of the streamflow loss from this section has been attributed to municipal groundwater withdrawals for El Paso and Ciudad Juarez (Miyamoto and others, 1995; Hibbs, 1999; Hibbs and others, 2003) and evapotranspiration (Miyamoto and others, 1995; Phillips and others, 2003; Eastoe and others, 2007).

Losses in the annual mean streamflow from the Rio Grande between San Marcial and El Paso have been documented in other studies. Stabler (1911) measured streamflow in the Rio Grande at San Marcial and El Paso from 1897 to 1908 (fig. 4) and found that the average difference in annual streamflow was 430 ft^3/s. The time period that Stabler (1911) monitored streamflow conditions was prior to the construction of Elephant Butte and Caballo Dams. Moore and Anderholm (2002) showed that during 1995 to 1997 the annual loss from the Rio Grande between San Marcial and Leasburg was 790 ft^3/s and that an additional 180 ft^3/s was lost between Leasburg and El Paso. One variable that confounds the direct comparison of annual streamflow conditions from time periods before and after the construction of Elephant Butte and Caballo Dams is the influence of storage and release of streamflow in these reservoirs. However, the

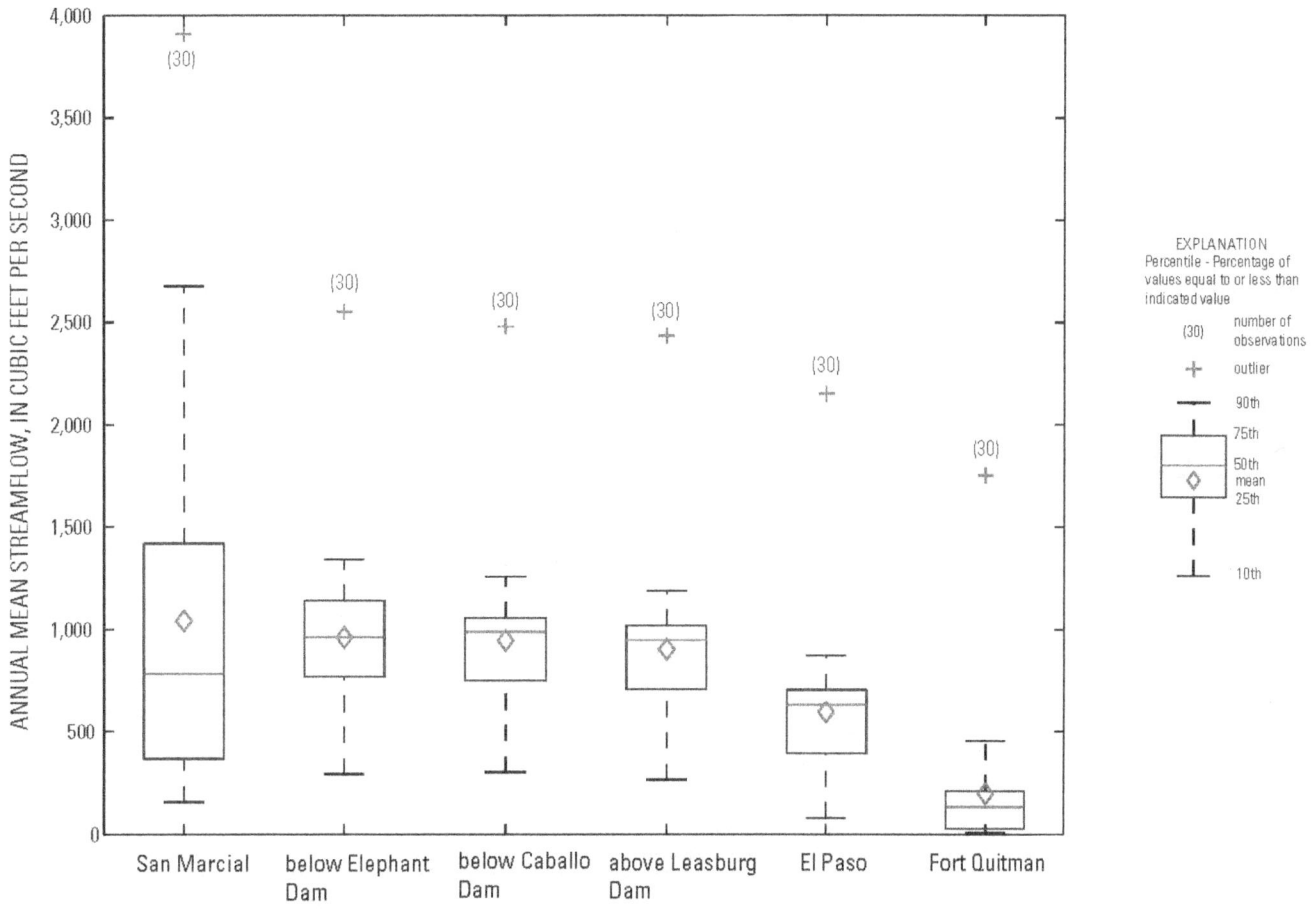

Figure 3. Annual mean streamflow measured at selected monitoring stations along the Rio Grande from 1934 to 1963 (data from Wilcox, 1968).

fact remains that as water is transported in the Rio Grande between San Marcial and El Paso, significant losses occur as a result of agricultural and riparian transpiration, evaporation, and seepage from the Rio Grande to the shallow alluvial aquifer (Stabler, 1911; Wilson and others, 1981; Moore and Anderholm, 2002).

Temporal Variability in Streamflow

Annual variation in the amount of streamflow that is transported down the Rio Grande is influenced by climate and the management of Elephant Butte and Caballo Reservoirs (fig. 5). Time-series data for annual mean streamflow for the Rio Grande at San Marcial shows a mix of wet and dry years between 1934 and 1963 (fig. 5A). The largest annual streamflow measured at San Marcial was 3,907 ft³/s in 1941, and the lowest annual streamflow of 151 ft³/s occurred in 1951. The influence that management of the Elephant Butte and Caballo Reservoirs has on streamflow in the Rio Grande is evident in the time-series records for the stations monitored by Wilcox (1968) below Elephant Butte Reservoir (fig. 5B).

Streamflow that passed San Marcial during wet years was used to increase water stored in Elephant Butte and Caballo Reservoirs, and a lesser amount was passed to downstream locations. Conversely, during dry years more water was released to downstream locations than the amount that entered Elephant Butte and Caballo Reservoirs. The extended drought period that occurred during the mid-1950s had substantial impacts on the water resources in the Rio Grande study area. The drought caused shortfalls in the amount of surface water available for irrigation in the Mesilla Basin and, as a result, many wells were drilled in an attempt to use groundwater to meet the irrigation demand (Leggat and others, 1962; Frenzel and others, 1992). Additionally, West (1995) hypothesized that increased reliance on groundwater to meet water-supply needs in the Mesilla Basin resulted in increased stress on the underlying alluvial aquifer, which subsequently decreased the storage coefficient. This increased stress has resulted in a decrease in the annual flows below the reservoirs through an increase in the river and canal losses to the underlying alluvial aquifer (Helm, 1984; West 1995).

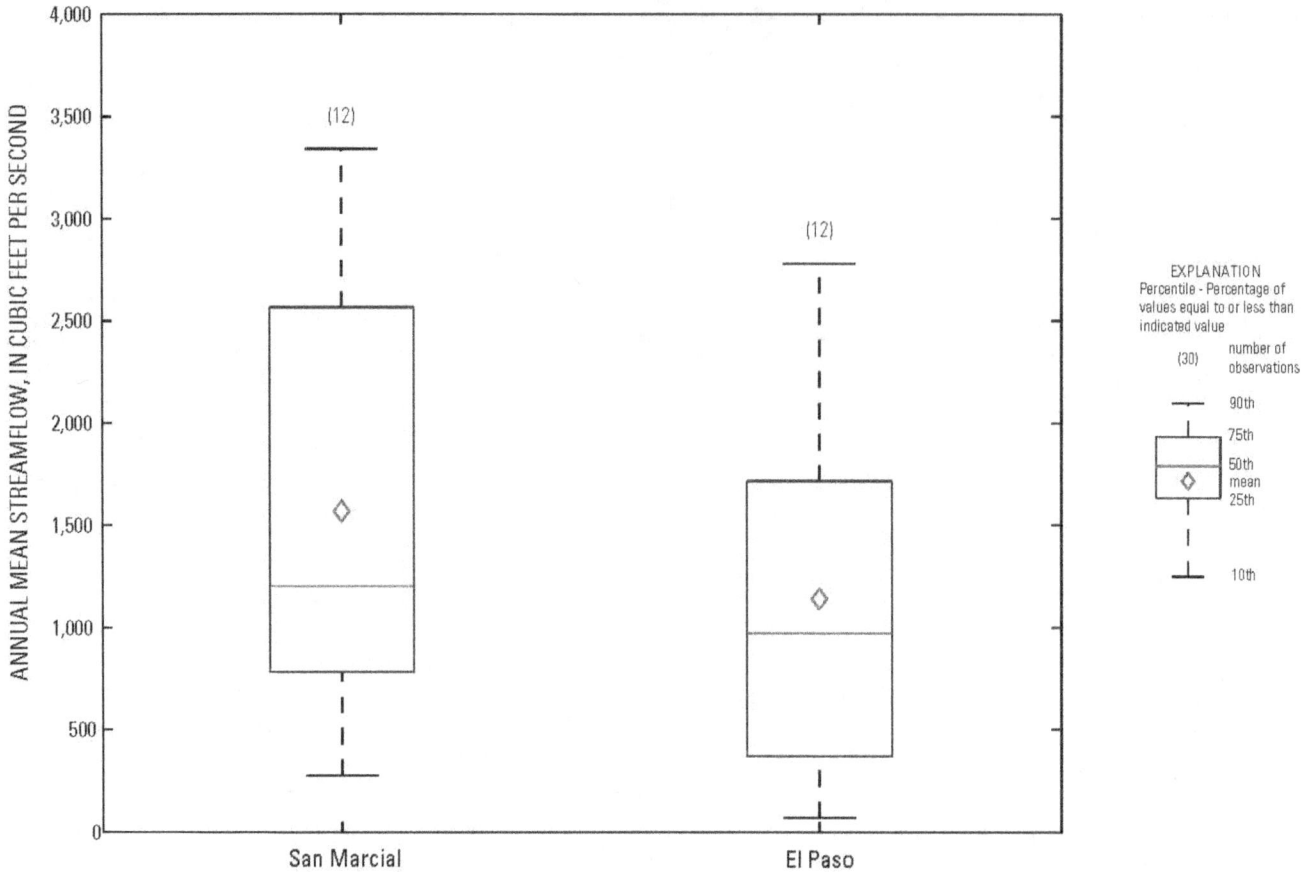

Figure 4. Boxplot of streamflow data collected from the Rio Grande at San Marcial and El Paso (Courchesne Bridge) from 1897 to 1908 by Stabler (1911).

Seasonal variation in streamflow in the Rio Grande in the study area, primarily a function of water management, is most evident at monitoring stations below Elephant Butte Reservoir (fig. 6). Two distinct water-management periods influence streamflow conditions in the Rio Grande study area. These seasons are generally categorized as irrigation and nonirrigation seasons (Wilcox, 1968). The irrigation season extends from March through September (roughly two-thirds of the year) and represents the period when water is being released from Elephant Butte and Caballo Reservoirs to supply water for the irrigation of agricultural crops. During this time period, streamflow in the Rio Grande between Elephant Butte Reservoir and El Paso is increased. Reductions in streamflow caused by evapotranspiration, surface-water diversions for irrigation, and leakage to the shallow alluvial aquifer occur in the Rio Grande between Leasburg and Fort Quitman. The nonirrigation season extends from October through February (roughly one-third of the year) and represents the time period when little to no water is released from the reservoirs. During this period, streamflow in the Rio Grande below Elephant Butte Reservoir is primarily inflow from agricultural drains (Wilcox, 1968), wastewater-treatment plants (Mills, 2003;

Moore and others, 2008), and groundwater discharge (Wilson and others, 1981; Ellis and others, 1993).

Summary of Streamflow Conditions

The spatial and temporal patterns in streamflow conditions provide information on the factors that govern streamflow along the Rio Grande study area. The management of Elephant Butte and Caballo Reservoirs is the primary factor that controls the spatial and temporal variability in Rio Grande streamflow conditions between Elephant Butte and El Paso. Additionally, losses have been attributed to evaporation from Elephant Butte and Caballo Reservoirs. Spatially, marked decreases in annual streamflow (approximately 700 ft³/s) occur between Leasburg and Fort Quitman (Appendix 1). These losses have been attributed to agricultural and riparian transpiration, municipal withdrawals, and seepage from the Rio Grande to the shallow alluvial aquifer. A strong temporal pattern is present in streamflow conditions along the Rio Grande. During the irrigation season, streamflow conditions between San Marcial and Leasburg are similar; however, streamflow decreases by a factor of seven in the Rio Grande

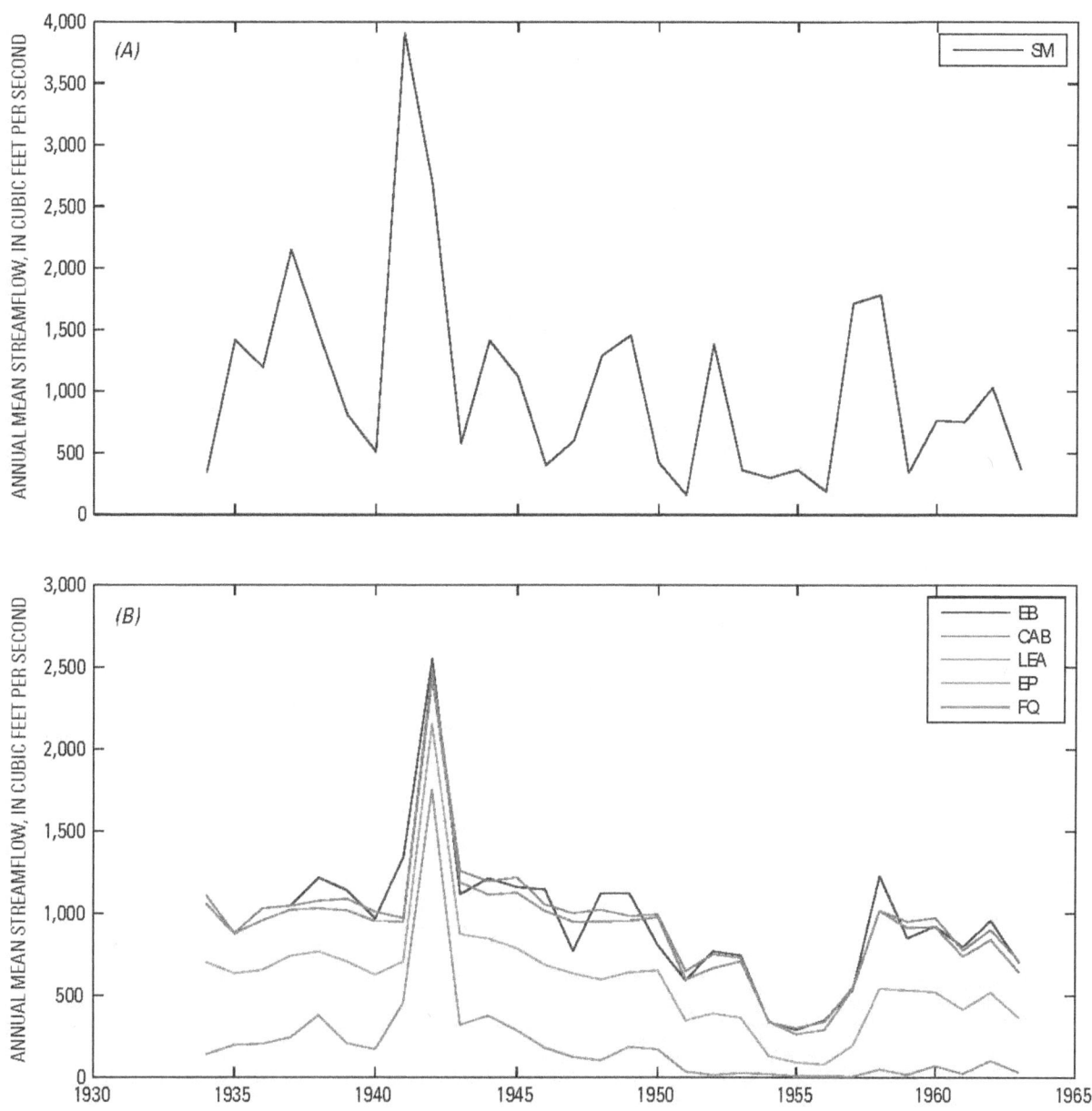

Figure 5. Plot of annual streamflow measured in the Rio Grande at (*A*) San Marcial and (*B*) below Elephant Butte Dam (EB), below Caballo Dam (CAB), above Leasburg Dam (LEA), at El Paso (EP) and at Fort Quitman (FQ) from 1934 to 1963 (Wilcox, 1968).

between Leasburg and Fort Quitman. This sevenfold decrease in streamflow has been primarily attributed to irrigation diversions, agricultural and riparian transpiration, and municipal withdrawals. During the nonirrigation season, streamflow entering Elephant Butte and Caballo Reservoirs is stored and not released to the downstream reaches. The pattern of increasing streamflow at stations downstream from Caballo Reservoir is a result of agricultural return flows, inflow of groundwater to the Rio Grande, and releases from wastewater-treatment facilities.

Dissolved-Solids Concentration

Dissolved-solids concentration data provide a good indicator of the general quality of surface water in the Rio Grande in the study area. Spatial and temporal patterns in dissolved-solids concentration data provide information pertaining to the potential sources and processes contributing to changes in concentrations. However, concentration data alone do not provide information on the mass of dissolved solids being transported downstream

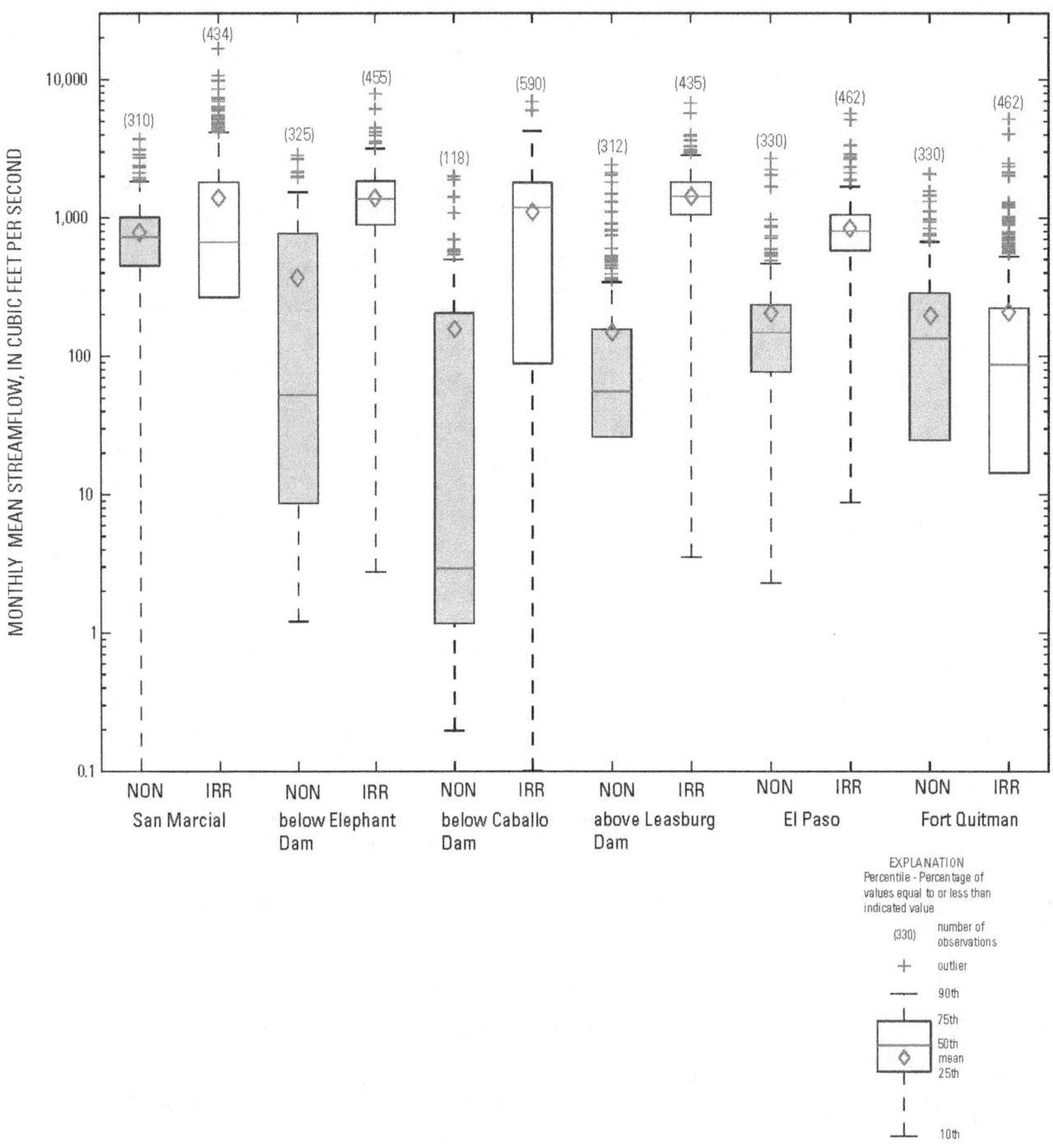

Figure 6.   Streamflow conditions during the nonirrigation (NON) and irrigation (IRR) season at selected sites in the Rio Grande study area from 1934 to 1999 (Wilcox, 1968; Williams, 2001).

Spatial Variability in Dissolved-Solids Concentration

The concentration of dissolved solids in the Rio Grande in the study area increases with distance downstream from Elephant Butte and Caballo Reservoirs (Lippincott, 1939; Moore and Anderholm, 2002; Phillips and others, 2003; Hogan and others, 2007; Moore and others, 2008; fig. 7). The range of dissolved-solids concentrations is similar for the Rio Grande at San Marcial, Elephant Butte, Caballo, and Leasburg. Average dissolved-solids concentration measured at the four stations from San Marcial to Leasburg ranged from 512 mg/L at Elephant Butte to 660 mg/L at Leasburg (fig. 7). Maximum dissolved-solids concentrations for these four stations ranged from 1,146 mg/L at Caballo to 1,861 at San Marcial (fig. 7). A marked increase in dissolved-solids concentration occurred in the Rio Grande between Leasburg and Fort Quitman. Average dissolved-solids concentration increased to 1,053 mg/L by the time the Rio Grande reaches El Paso and to 3,275 mg/L by the time the Rio Grande reached Fort Quitman (fig. 7). Maximum dissolved-solids concentrations in the Rio

Grande at El Paso and Fort Quitman were 3,831 mg/L and 10,738 mg/L, respectively. Essentially, the concentration of dissolved solids in the Rio Grande (considering both irrigation and nonirrigation seasons) doubles from Elephant Butte to El Paso and increases by more than a factor of five from Elephant Butte to Fort Quitman. The increases in dissolved-solids concentration between Elephant Butte and El Paso have been attributed to the inflow of saline groundwater at the distal end of the Palomas Basin (Wilson and others, 1981; Anderholm, 2002) and Mesilla Basin (Wilson and others, 1981; Phillips and others, 2003; Witcher and others, 2004). The increase in dissolved-solids concentration between El Paso and Fort Quitman has been attributed to the inflow of saline groundwater near the El Paso-Hudspeth County line (Hibbs and Merino, 2007).

The variation in dissolved-solids concentration in the Rio Grande in the study area has been documented since the early 1900s. Stabler (1911) showed that the average dissolved-solids concentrations in the Rio Grande between 1905 and 1907, prior to the construction of the Elephant Butte and Caballo Dams, were 404 mg/L and 681 mg/L at San Marcial

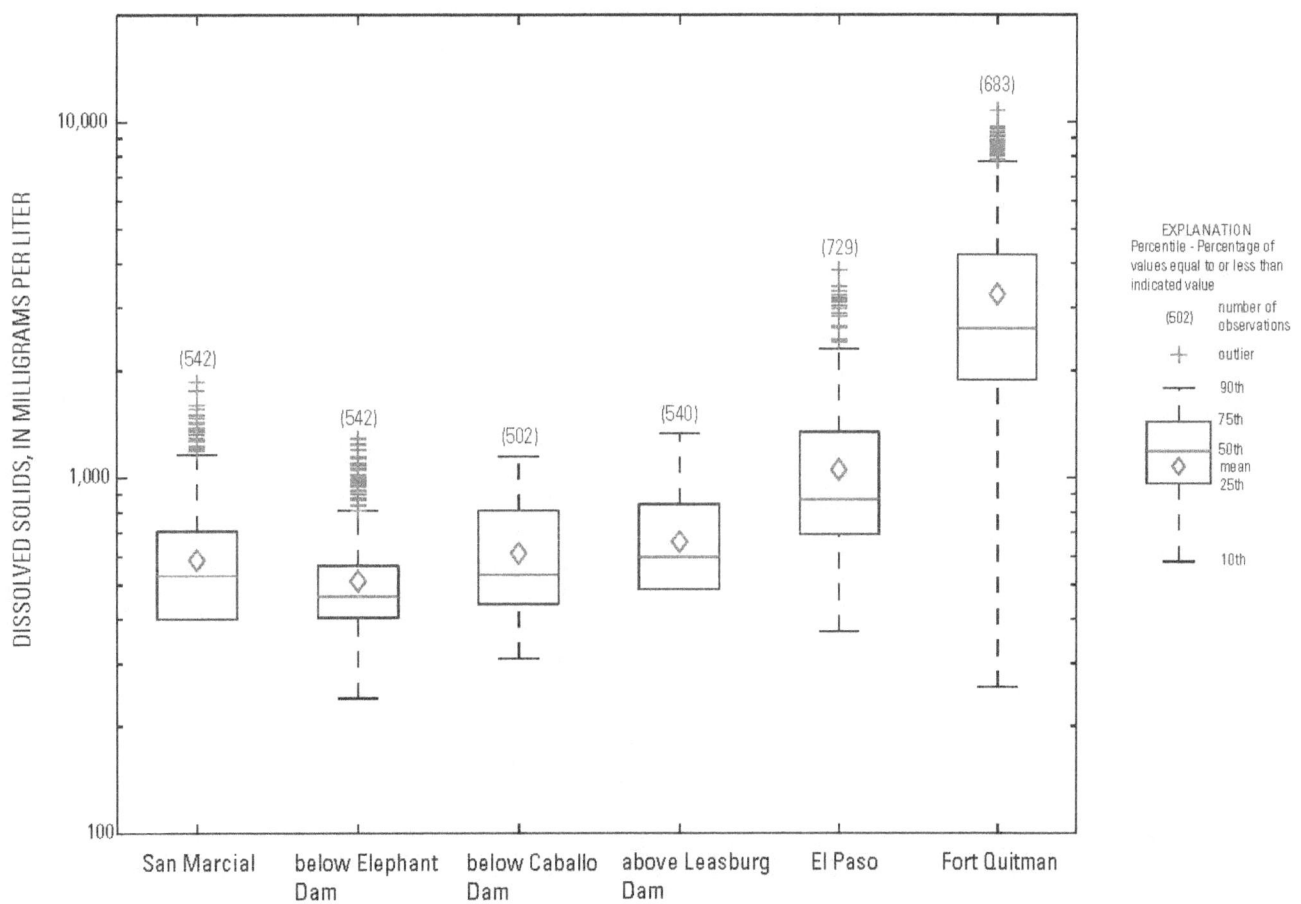

Figure 7. Dissolved-solids concentration at selected sites in the Rio Grande study area from 1934 to 1999 (Wilcox, 1968; Williams, 2001).

and El Paso, respectively. Water-quality data collected by Stabler (1911) show that the maximum dissolved-solids concentrations measured at San Marcial and El Paso were 1,930 mg/L and 3,880 mg/L, respectively. Lippincott (1939) indicated that the concentration of dissolved solids in the Rio Grande was 427 mg/L at the head of Elephant Butte Reservoir, 832 mg/L at El Paso, and 2,120 mg/L at Fort Quitman. Monthly dissolved-solids concentration data collected by Moore and Anderholm (2002) during 1993–95 revealed that the concentration of dissolved solids increased by 200 mg/L between Leasburg and El Paso.

Starting in 2000, researchers from the Sustainability of Semi-Arid Hydrology and Riparian Areas (SAHRA) National Science Foundation Science and Technology Center (http://www.sahra.arizona.edu/) started a water-quality monitoring program to evaluate changes in water-quality conditions and identify contributing sources at a fine spatial scale along the Rio Grande from the headwaters in Colorado to Fort Quitman, Texas (Phillips and others, 2003; Hogan and others, 2007). Water-quality monitoring was performed

twice a year, once during winter (nonirrigation season) and once during the summer (irrigation season). Results from this monitoring effort indicated that dissolved-solids concentration in the Rio Grande increased by nearly two orders of magnitude from the headwaters in Colorado to Fort Quitman, Texas (fig. 8). Dissolved-solids concentration increased noticeably at the upstream end of the Rio Grande study area at San Acacia (655 km). The largest increase in dissolved-solids concentration occurred just above El Paso (1,015 km) and continued to Fort Quitman (fig. 8). Additionally, marked increases in the concentration of dissolved solids commonly coincide with contributions from agricultural drains, municipal wastewater-treatment plants, and direct groundwater discharge at the distal ends of the alluvial-fill basins (Mills, 2003; Phillips and others, 2003; Lacey, 2006; Hogan and others, 2007; Bastien, 2009). Other studies have found that the concentration of dissolved solids in the agricultural drains is commonly two to three times greater than the dissolved-solids concentration in the Rio Grande (Anderholm, 2002; Bastien, 2009).

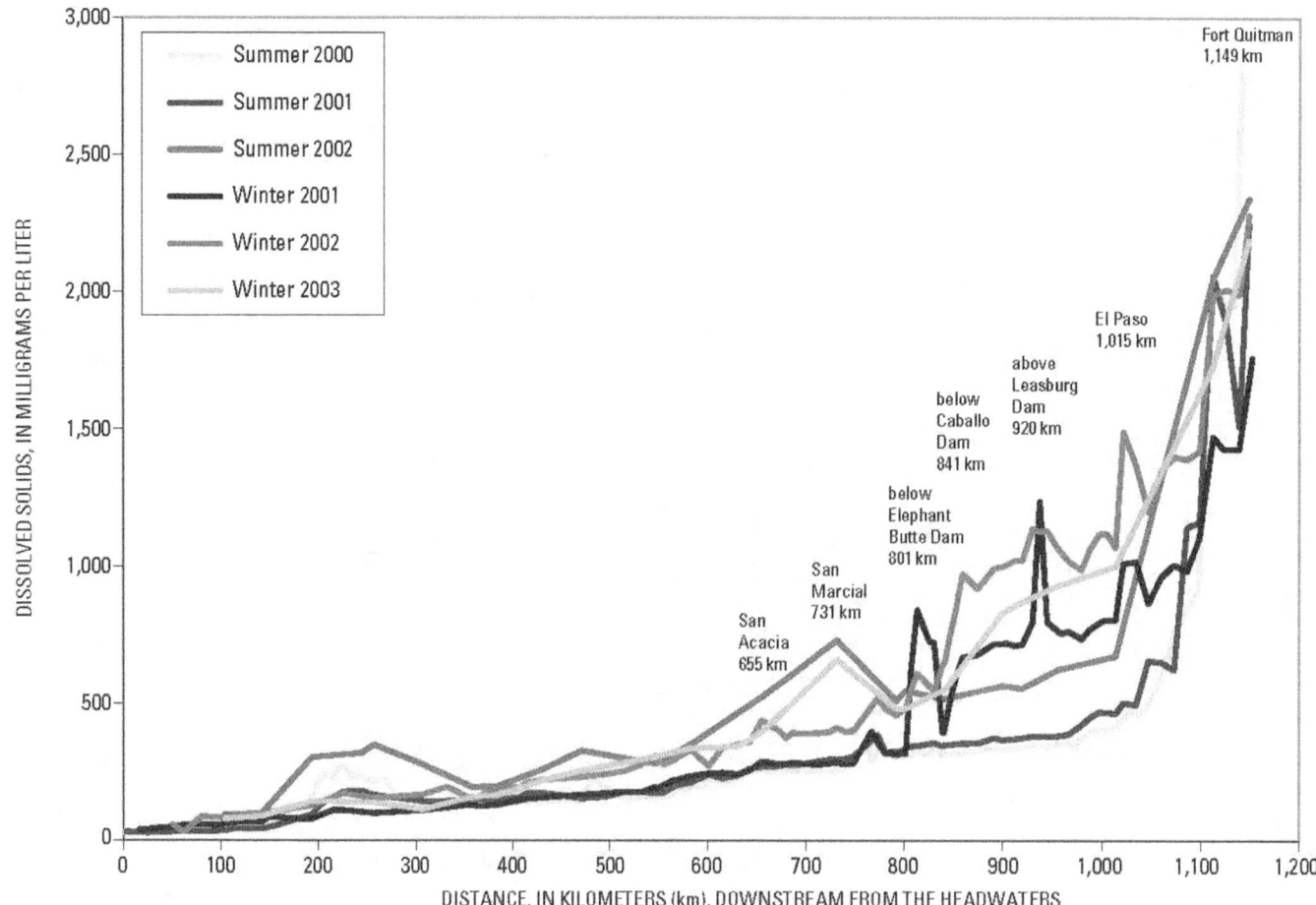

Figure 8.   Plot of dissolved-solids concentration collected during the winter and summer 2000–3 from the headwaters in Colorado to Fort Quitman, Texas (Phillips and others, 2003; Hogan and others, 2007).

Temporal Variability in Dissolved-Solids Concentration

Annual variation in the concentration of dissolved solids in the Rio Grande is influenced by changes in the Rio Grande hydrology (Yuan and Miyamoto, 2004) and the contributions from the various sources of dissolved solids. Year-to-year changes in the concentration of dissolved solids in the Rio Grande were identified by applying a smooth-fit curve analytical technique (locally weighted scatter plot smoothing (LOWESS); Helsel and Hirsch, 1992) to data collected by Wilcox (1968) and compiled by Williams (2001) at San Marcial, El Paso, and Fort Quitman (fig. 9). The LOWESS curve follows the trend in the observed data. The extended drought period of the 1950s can be identified by elevated dissolved-solids concentrations at all three stations (fig. 9). Similar temporal patterns in dissolved-solids concentrations occurred at San Marcial and El Paso; conversely, the patterns in dissolved-solids concentration were considerably different between El Paso and Fort Quitman (fig. 9). The LOWESS curves for San Marcial and El Paso also indicate that the concentrations of dissolved solids at these two sites have been decreasing since the drought period of the 1950s; similarly, dissolved-solids concentrations at Fort Quitman have been decreasing since the late 1970s.

Seasonal variation in dissolved-solids concentration in the Rio Grande is influenced primarily by the amount of water that is transported. Concentration of dissolved solids are considerably elevated in the Rio Grande at Caballo and El Paso during the nonirrigation season (fig. 10). During the nonirrigation season, streamflow is the lowest; as a result, dissolved solids in water transported from agricultural drains, direct groundwater discharge, and municipal wastewater-treatment plants are not diluted (Moore and others, 2008; fig. 10). Conversely, during the irrigation season, dissolved-solids concentrations at these same stations are maintained at a considerably lower level because the increased streamflow levels in the Rio Grande dilute the concentration of dissolved

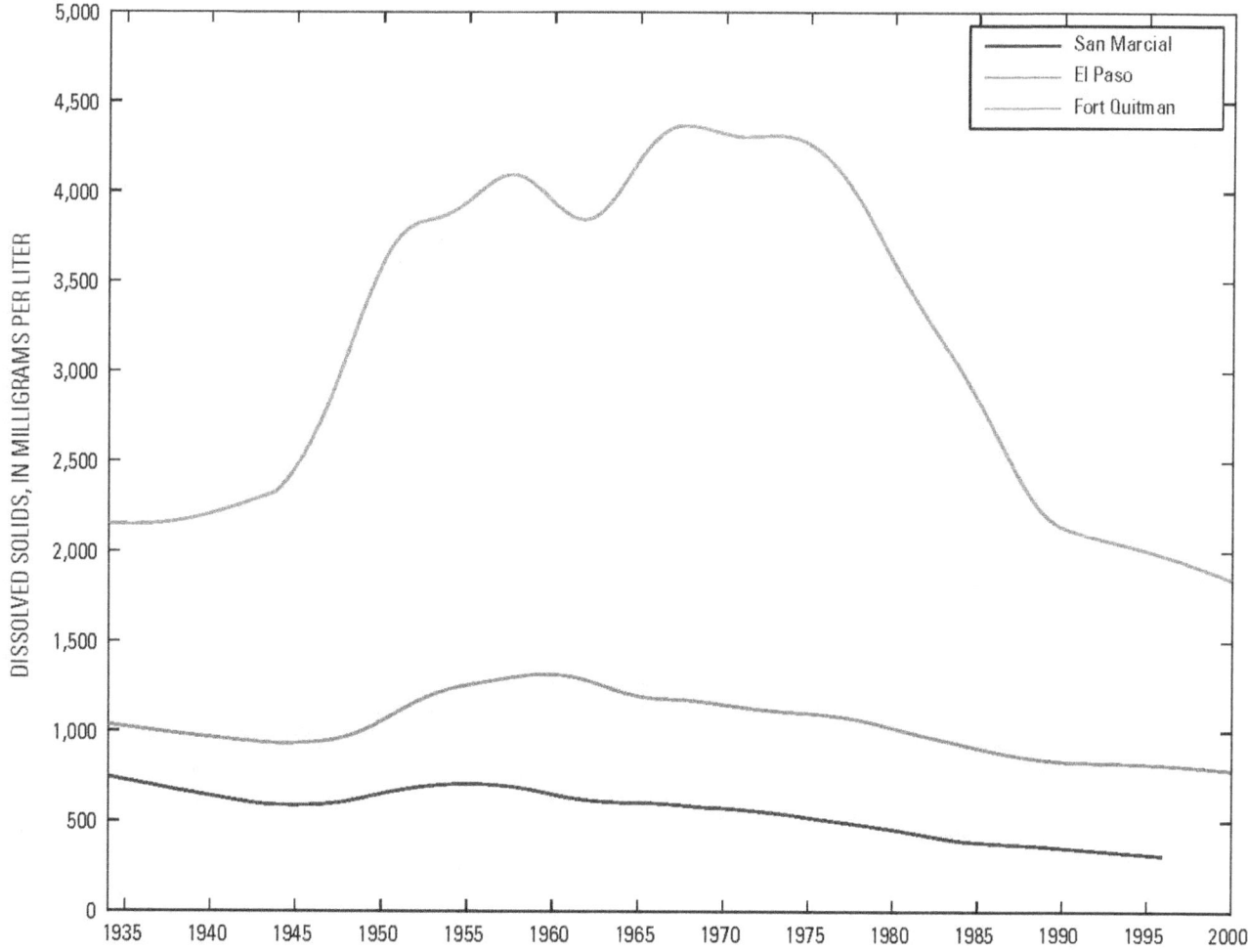

Figure 9. Locally weighted scatter plot smoothing curve from the Rio Grande at San Marcial, El Paso, and Fort Quitman

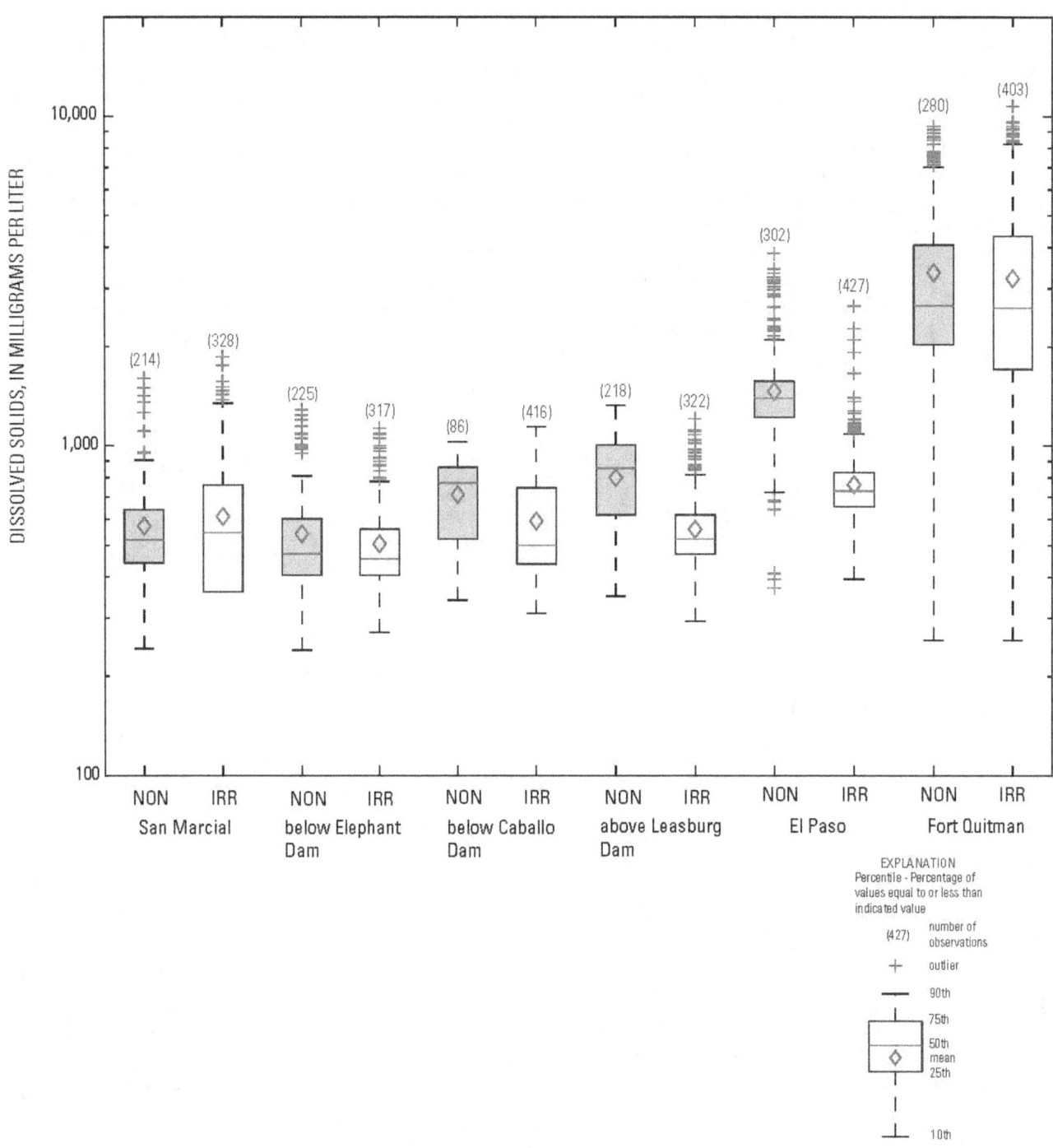

Figure 10. Dissolved-solids concentration during the nonirrigation (NON) and irrigation (IRR) seasons at selected sites in the Rio Grande study area from 1934 to 1999 (Wilcox, 1968; Williams, 2001).

solids inflowing from agricultural drains, direct groundwater discharge, and municipal wastewater-treatment plants (Moore and others, 2008; fig. 10). Conversely, seasonal variability in dissolved-solids concentration at San Marcial and Fort Quitman is minimal and is related to the relatively minor seasonal variability in streamflow exhibited at both of these stations compared to other stations.

Spatial and Temporal Variability in Ion Composition

In addition to the spatial and temporal variations in dissolved solids, the concentrations of the individual solute species that comprise the dissolved solids also vary spatially and temporally. The piper diagram (Piper, 1944) is a useful tool to evaluate the major-ion composition of water samples. Bastien (2009) used the piper diagram to describe the major-ion composition of the Rio Grande at Otowi, New Mexico (Otowi); Rio Grande at San Marcial, New Mexico (San Marcial); and Rio Grande at El Paso, Texas (El Paso). Bastien (2009) showed how the ion composition of the Rio Grande water evolves as it is transported from Otowi to El Paso and how this ionic transformation varied during the past century. The ion composition of the Rio Grande evolves from calcium-bicarbonate water near the Colorado and New Mexico border (Otowi) to sodium-sulfate-chloride water near El Paso (fig. 11). The chemical composition of the water in the Rio Grande at Otowi is influenced primarily by the water delivered by headwater tributaries; whereas, the chemical compositions of the water in the Rio Grande at San Marcial and El Paso are influenced primarily by the inflow of saline groundwater (Bastien (2009). Sodium-sulfate-chloride water is an evolved hydrochemical facies that typically is found in saline groundwater.

The ionic composition of the water in the Rio Grande at El Paso has varied over time (fig. 12). The ionic composition of the water in the Rio Grande at El Paso prior to the construction of the Elephant Butte Dam (Stabler, 1911) closely matches the ionic composition of the water in the Rio Grande at San Marcial (Bastien, 2009; fig. 11). Following the construction of Elephant Butte Dam, the composition of calcium and carbonate in the Rio Grande was reduced because of carbonate mineral precipitation in Elephant Butte Reservoir (Bastien, 2009; fig. 12). Additionally, the concentration of sulfate, chloride, and sodium increased in the Rio Grande below Elephant Butte Reservoir because of increased inflow from saline groundwater accompanied by precipitation of the more reactive ions (calcium, magnesium, and bicarbonate) under agricultural fields (Bastien, 2009; fig. 12). During the most recent decades, the composition of the anions (chloride, sulfate, bicarbonate plus carbonate) in the Rio Grande at El Paso has been shifting closer to the anion composition observed by Stabler (1911) prior to Elephant Butte (Bastien, 2009; fig. 12). Additional information on the ion composition of surface water and groundwater within the Rio Grande study area can be found in Wilson and others (1981) and Frenzel and others (1992).

Summary of Dissolved-Solids Concentrations

The spatial and temporal patterns exhibited in dissolved-solids concentration data provide information on the factors that influence salinity in the Rio Grande. Spatial patterns exhibited in dissolved-solids concentration data indicate that concentrations increase with increasing distance downstream from San Acacia, New Mexico (Appendix 1). This pattern of increasing concentration is apparent in dissolved-solids concentration data extending as far back as the early 1900s. The most dramatic increase in dissolved-solids concentrations occurs in the Rio Grande between Leasburg and Fort Quitman where average concentrations increase by a factor of five (612 to 3,275 mg/L). The locations where dissolved-solids concentrations increase most noticeably (San Acacia, San Marcial, Elephant Butte, Leasburg, and El Paso) coincide with the distal ends of the associated underlying alluvial basins where the inflow of saline groundwater is the primary factor influencing dissolved-solids concentration.

Temporal patterns in dissolved-solids concentration data along the Rio Grande between 1934 and 1999 reveal much information regarding the impact of climate and water-management operations on dissolved-solids concentration. Above Elephant Butte Reservoir, dissolved-solids concentrations are similar for the irrigation and nonirrigation seasons, which indicates that streamflow and contributing sources of dissolved solids are consistent from season to season (Appendix 1). From Elephant Butte to El Paso, dissolved-solids concentrations exhibit significant temporal variation. During the nonirrigation season when streamflow is substantially reduced, dissolved-solids concentrations nearly triple (from about 500 to 1,500 mg/L); this increase has been attributed primarily to the inflow of groundwater containing elevated dissolved-solids concentration and municipal wastewater-treatment facilities. During the nonirrigation season when streamflow is increased, dissolved-solids concentrations are comparable (about 500 to 600 mg/L) and substantially reduced compared to concentrations during the nonirrigation season. The increased streamflow during this period serves to dilute the dissolved solids delivered through the inflow of groundwater and municipal wastewater-treatment facilities. Therefore, the primary factors that control dissolved-solids concentrations in the Rio Grande between Elephant Butte and El Paso are water-management operations and the inflow of saline groundwater. Below El Paso, dissolved-solids concentrations in the Rio Grande increase to an average concentration of 2,500 mg/L by the time the water reaches Fort Quitman during both the irrigation and nonirrigation seasons. The primary factor influencing dissolved-solids concentrations in the Rio Grande between El Paso and Fort Quitman is inflow of saline groundwater near the El Paso-Hudspeth County line.

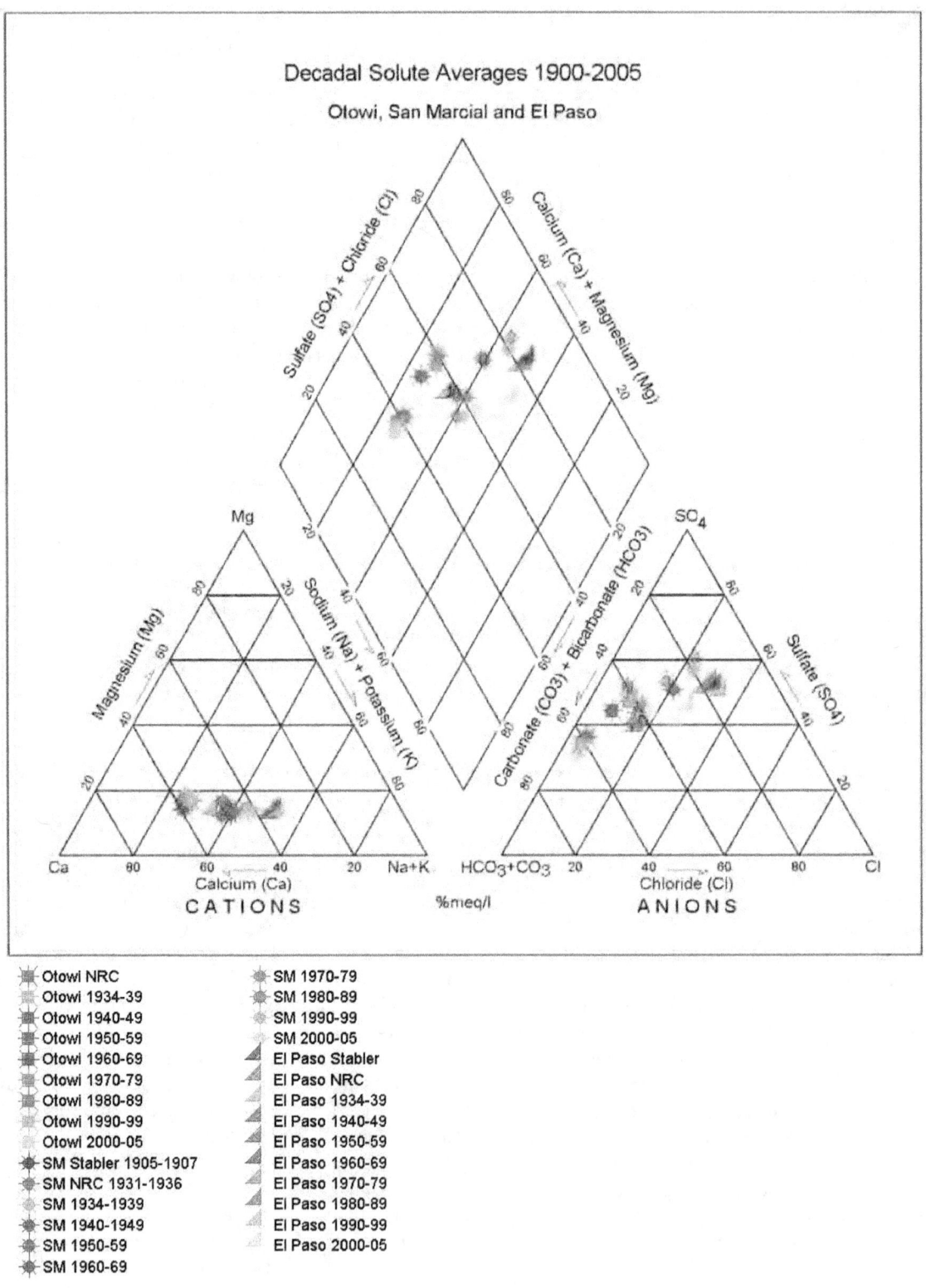

Figure 11.   Piper diagram of average decadal chemistry from the decades 1905–2000 for three Rio Grande stations: Otowi, San Marcial, and El Paso (Bastien, 2009; used with permission).

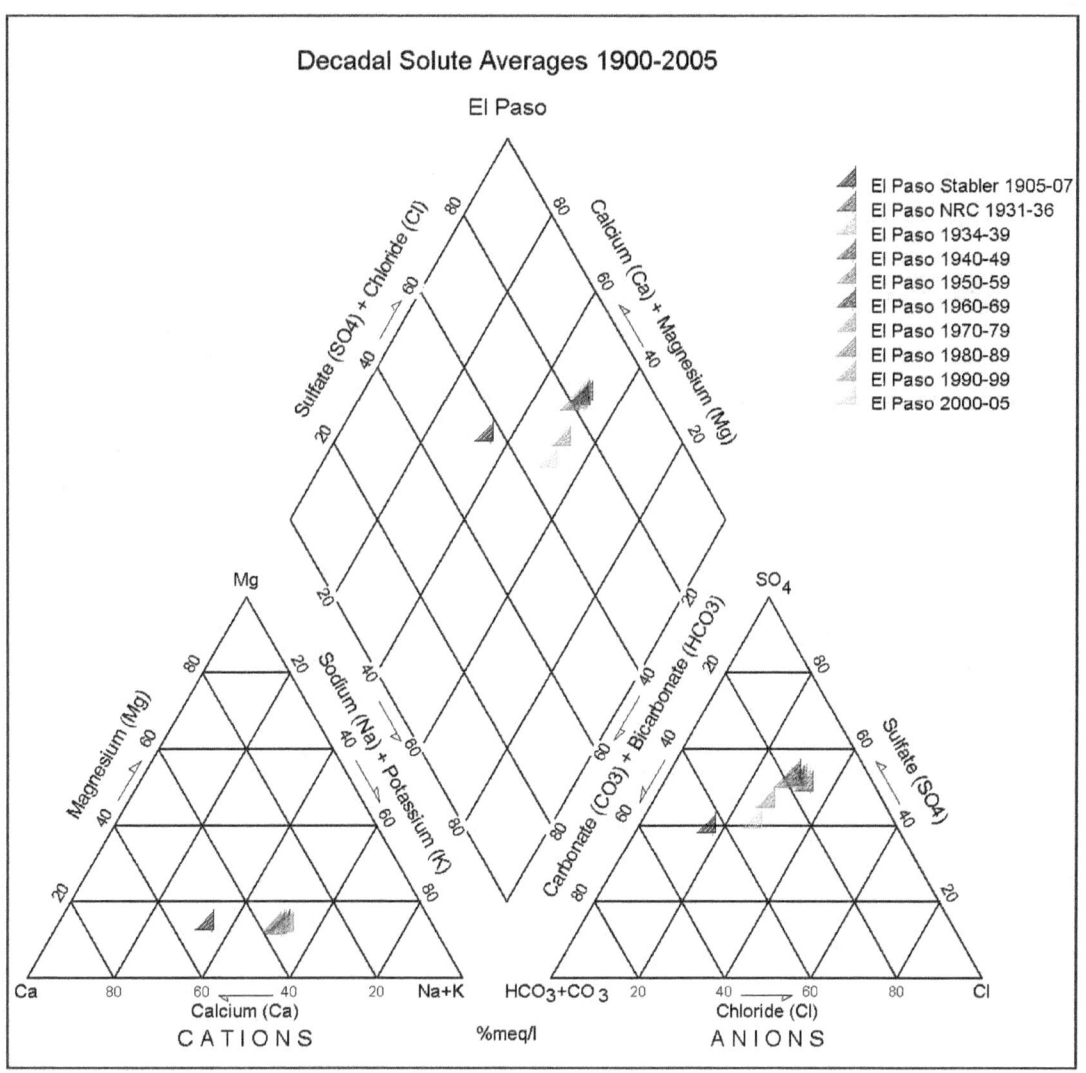

Figure 12.   Piper diagram of average decadal chemistry of water samples collected from the Rio Grande at El Paso for the decades 1905–2000 (Bastien, 2009; used with permission).

Dissolved-Solids Loads

Dissolved-solids load data provide important information pertaining to the mass of dissolved solids that are transported down the Rio Grande. Load, or burden, is defined as the mass of a given water-quality constituent transported during a given time period. Therefore, the load of a given constituent is a function of both concentration and flow. Dissolved-solids loads will only increase when new mass of dissolved solids is added through sources, such as direct groundwater discharge, tributary inflow, and discharge from municipal wastewater-treatment plants (Moore and Anderholm, 2002). Dissolved-solids loads will only decrease when mass is removed from the system through pathways, such as irrigation diversions, groundwater recharge (seepage), or by precipitation of relatively insoluble minerals (Moore and Anderholm, 2002).

The calculation of loads for dissolved solids in the Rio Grande in the study area is a critical step for the establishment of a budget for dissolved-solids transport. Various methods have been used to calculate dissolved-solids loads. Instantaneous loads are calculated by multiplying the concentration from a single water-quality sample by the streamflow that occurred when the sample was collected. Instantaneous loads are particularly useful for developing a detailed mass-balance of solute transport for a single point in time. Mills (2003), Phillips and others (2003), and Hogan and others (2007) used instantaneous loads to determine the mass balance for chloride transport in the Rio Grande from the headwaters in Colorado to Fort Quitman, Texas, during winter and summer hydrologic conditions. Time-integrated loads (for example, daily, monthly, annual, and decadal) are calculated using one of two methods: (1) multiplying an average water-quality concentration for a given time period by the total streamflow that occurred during that time period and a unit conversion factor (Wilcox, 1968; Bastien, 2009); or (2) applying a multiple linear-regression model to relate a water-quality constituent to a given streamflow condition (Moore and Anderholm, 2002). The benefit of using time-integrated loads is that they account for variations in flow and water-quality conditions. The discussion on loads in the Rio Grande study area will focus solely on time-integrated loads calculated by Wilcox (1968) and Moore and Anderholm (2002).

Spatial Variability in Dissolved-Solids Loads

Dissolved-solids loads in the Rio Grande study area generally increase from San Marcial to Leasburg and decrease from Leasburg to Fort Quitman (Witcher and others, 2004; fig. 13). The mean daily load for dissolved solids during 1934-63 was 1,295 tons/d at San Marcial and 1,364 tons/d at Leasburg (an increase of 69 tons/d). Both streamflow and dissolved-solids concentrations increase between San Marcial and Leasburg, indicating that the increase in load is caused

by inflow of saline groundwater (Phillips and others, 2004; Hogan and others, 2007). The average daily load decreased by 196 tons in the Rio Grande between Leasburg and El Paso during 1934–63 (Wilcox, 1968). Between Leasburg and El Paso, annual streamflow is reduced, on average, by nearly 40 percent; however, the annual load for dissolved solids, on average, is reduced by only 13 percent. The minor reduction of dissolved-solids load relative to the losses in streamflow between Leasburg and El Paso reflects the increased dissolved solids derived from the discharge of agricultural drains, municipal wastewater-treatment plants, and saline groundwater within this reach (Mills, 2003; Moore and others, 2008). More recent data from this reach (Moore and Anderholm, 2002) indicates that during 1993–95, the mean daily load in the Rio Grande between Leasburg and El Paso increased by 138 tons/d even though streamflow decreased by 213 ft^3/s. Between El Paso and Fort Quitman, the mean daily load in the Rio Grande decreased by 252 tons/d (Wilcox, 1968). Within this reach of the Rio Grande, approximately 70 percent of the streamflow was lost between El Paso and Fort Quitman; however, the mean daily load was only reduced by 22 percent (Wilcox, 1968). If the reduction in dissolved-solids

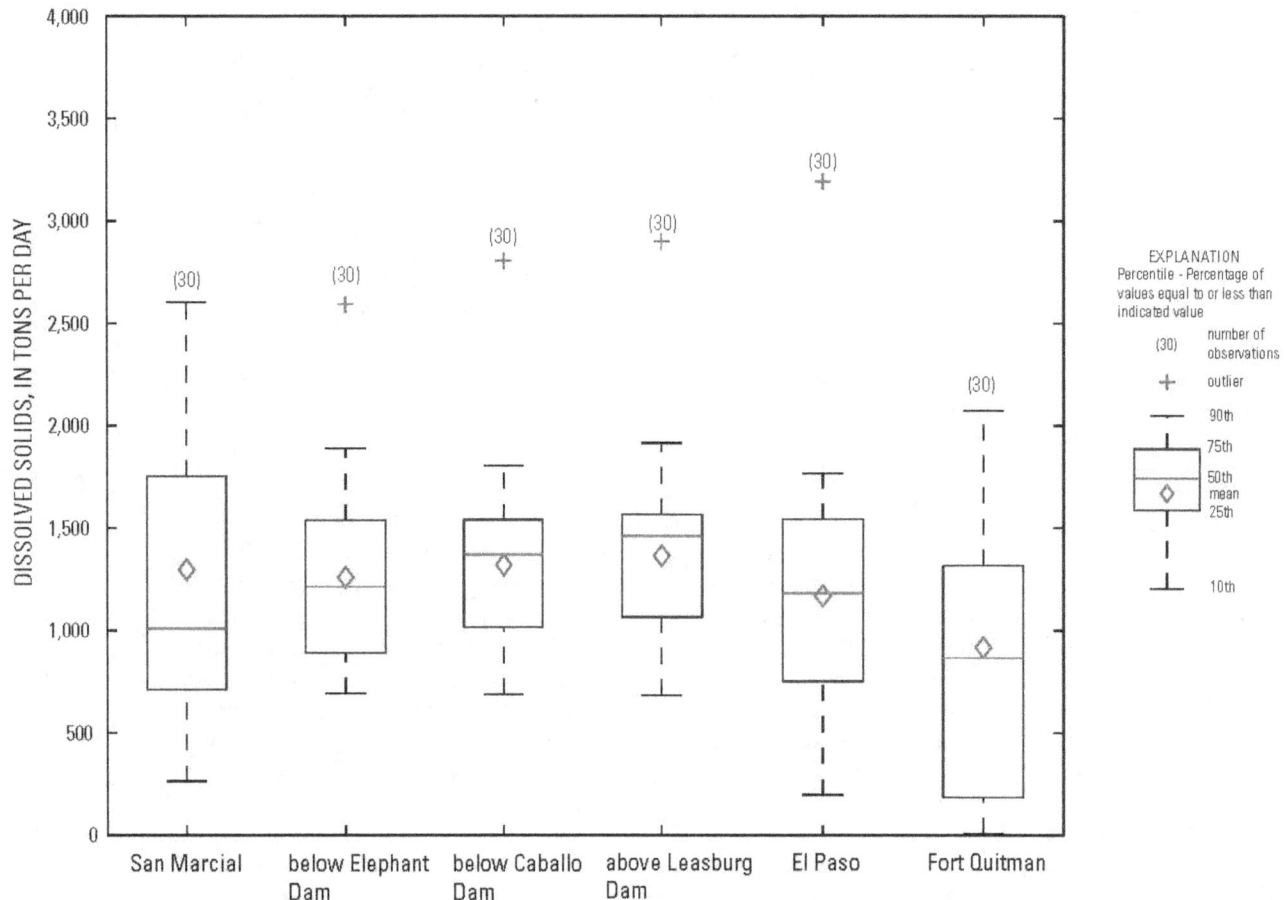

Figure 13. Boxplot of dissolved-solids annual mean daily loads for selected stations along the Rio Grande study area during 1934–63 (Wilcox, 1968).

loads was a result of the loss in streamflow, then the total reduction in dissolved solids would be nearly 70 percent. However, the dissolved-solids load is only decreased by 22 percent, which indicates that a source of water with elevated concentrations of dissolved solids is contributing dissolved solids to the Rio Grande between El Paso and Fort Quitman. Hibbs and Merino (2007) determined that inflowing saline groundwater near the El Paso-Hudspeth County line is the dominant source of dissolved solids between El Paso and Fort Quitman.

Temporal Variability in Dissolved-Solids Loads

Annual variation in the mass of dissolved solids that are transported down the Rio Grande is influenced by climate and the management of Elephant Butte and Caballo Reservoirs (fig. 14). Investigation of time-series data for the annual mean load of dissolved solids transported in the Rio Grande at San Marcial shows the influence that climate had on the transport of dissolved solids during 1934–63 (fig. 14A). During wet years the load of dissolved solids in the Rio Grande at San

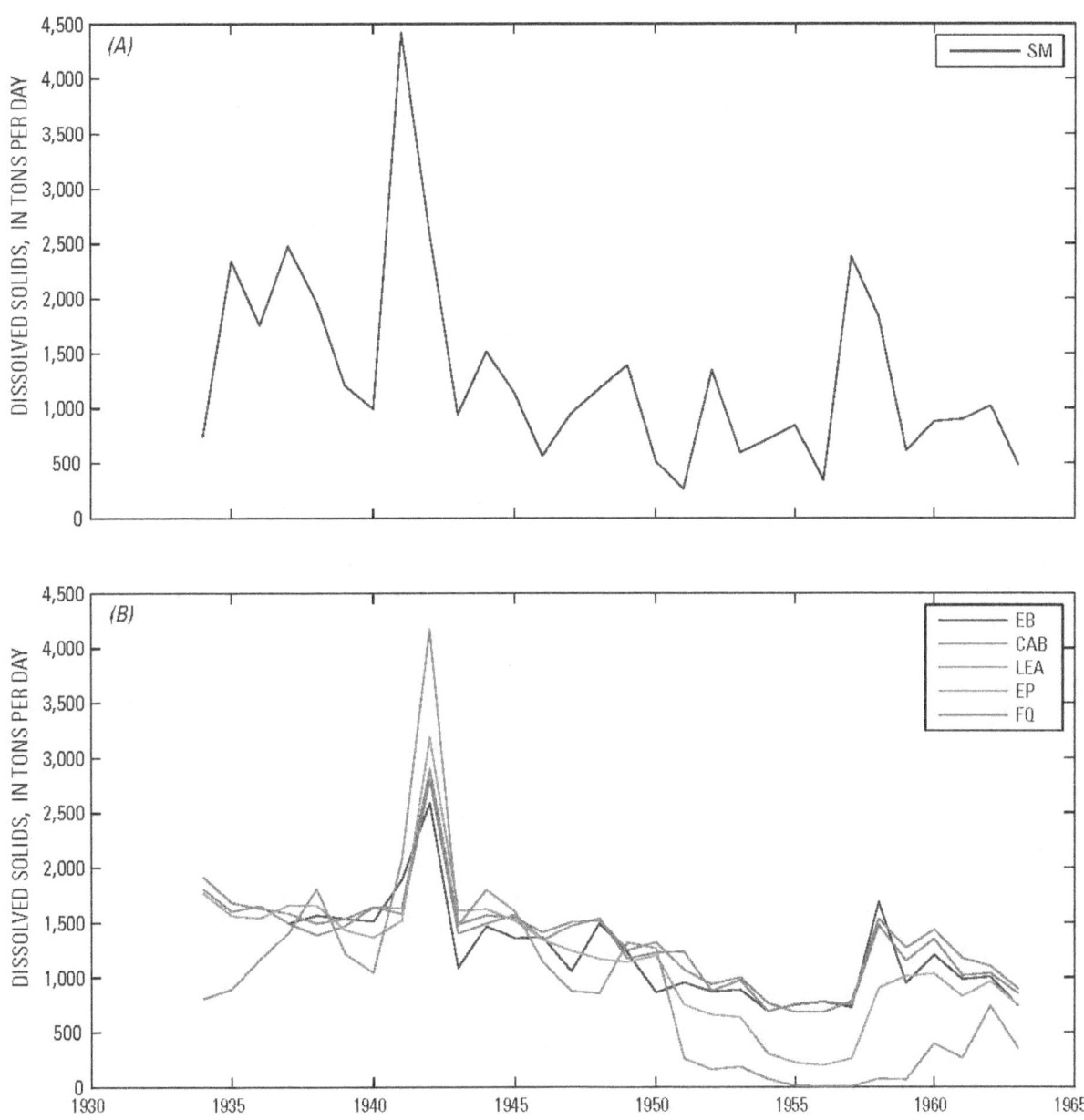

Figure 14.   Plot of dissolved-solids annual mean loads measured in the Rio Grande at (A) San Marcial and (B) below Elephant Butte Dam (EB), below Caballo Dam (CAB), above Leasburg Dam (LEA), at El Paso (EP), and at Fort Quitman (FQ) from 1934 to 1963 (Wilcox, 1968).

Marcial increased, and during drier years the load decreased. The influence of management of the Elephant Butte and Caballo Reservoirs on the load of dissolved solids in the Rio Grande is evident in the time-series records for the stations monitored by Wilcox (1968) below Elephant Butte Reservoir (fig. 14B). In general, most of the load of dissolved solids that passes San Marcial during wet years is stored in Elephant Butte and Caballo Reservoirs and a lesser amount is passed to downstream locations. Conversely, during drier years, more water and associated dissolved-solid load are released to downstream locations than enter Elephant Butte and Caballo Reservoirs. The influence of the extended drought during the 1950s on dissolved-solids load in the Rio Grande below Elephant Butte Reservoir is evident in figure 14B; dissolved-solids loads were considerably reduced in the Rio Grande at El Paso and Fort Quitman. The downstream reduction in dissolved-solids loads in the Rio Grande is primarily a result of the storage of dissolved solids in the irrigated soils and(or) underlying alluvial aquifer (Miyamoto and others, 1995; Moore and Anderholm, 2002).

Seasonal variation in dissolved-solids loads in the Rio Grande is influenced primarily by the amount of water that is being transported. The management of Elephant Butte and Caballo Reservoirs has a major influence on the seasonal variation of the downstream transport of dissolved solids. These reservoirs store dissolved solids during the nonirrigation season, and a portion of these dissolved solids is released during the irrigation season. Dissolved-solids loads in the Rio Grande are greatest during the irrigation season. During the irrigation season, the load of dissolved solids increases between San Marcial and Leasburg (fig. 15). This increase in load during the irrigation season can be attributed to dissolved solids that are transported into the study area by snowmelt runoff and released from Elephant Butte and Caballo Reservoirs. Additional increases in dissolved-solids loads in the Rio Grande between San Marcial and Leasburg have been attributed to the inflow of regional groundwater with increased concentrations of dissolved solids (Cox and Reeder, 1962; Anderholm, 2002). During the nonirrigation season, dissolved-solids loads in the Rio Grande below Elephant Butte Reservoir are reduced considerably because of limited streamflow; however, the pattern of increasing loads along the Rio Grande between Caballo and El Paso during the nonirrigation season has been attributed to contributions from agricultural drains, municipal wastewater-treatment plants, and discharge of saline groundwater (Mills, 2003; Moore and others, 2008; fig. 15).

Summary of Dissolved-Solids Loads

The value of understanding the spatial and temporal patterns in dissolved-solids loads is that these data provide a direct measure of the mass of dissolved solids that is transported or stored within a given reach of the Rio Grande. Spatially, dissolved-solids loads exhibit two distinct patterns

(Appendix 1). The first pattern is one of slightly increasing loads between San Marcial and Leasburg. This pattern indicates that there is a net downstream flux of dissolved solids (that is, the mass of dissolved solids being transported exceeds the mass being stored), and that the mass of new load (for example, groundwater discharge) entering the reach exceeds the mass of load being stored (for example, groundwater recharge). The second pattern is one of decreasing dissolved-solids load in the Rio Grande between Leasburg and Fort Quitman. This pattern indicates that more dissolved solids are being stored through processes, such as irrigation diversions, groundwater recharge, municipal water supply, and mineral interactions, than are being transported downstream. Annual variations in dissolved-solids loads at monitoring stations above and below Elephant Butte Reservoir show that climate and management of Elephant Butte Reservoir considerably influence the downstream flux of dissolved solids. During wet years, Elephant Butte Reservoir typically stores dissolved solids along with streamflow; whereas, during dry years, Elephant Butte Reservoir releases stored dissolved solids to downstream reaches. During the irrigation season, dissolved-solids loads are high because of increased streamflow and show a negative trend from Leasburg to Fort Quitman because of increased storage by processes that include irrigation diversions, municipal water supply, and agricultural and riparian transpiration. During the nonirrigation season, dissolved-solid loads are lower because of decreased streamflow and show a positive trend from Caballo to Fort Quitman. This positive trend is a direct result of new dissolved solids entering the Rio Grande from the inflow of saline groundwater, agricultural drains, and wastewater-treatment plants.

Dissolved-Solids Flow-Weighted Concentrations

Flow-weighted concentrations have been used by the Colorado River Salinity Management Program to establish water-quality goals and evaluate progress in meeting those goals (Colorado River Basin Salinity Control Forum, 2008). The flow-weighted concentration is an estimate of the mean annual concentration in a total volume of water flowing past a specific location during a specific time period, such as a month or a year (Langland and others, 2006). The flow-weighted concentration (milligrams per liter) is calculated by dividing the total monthly or annual load by the total monthly or annual flow. The Colorado River Project (Colorado River Basin Salinity Control Forum, 2008) established water-quality criteria for dissolved-solids concentration at three monitoring stations along the Colorado River (fig. 16). The established criteria for dissolved-solids concentration at each monitoring station is based on a flow-weighted concentration. The annual flow-weighted concentration at each station is used to evaluate progress towards the goal of reducing dissolved-solids loads in the Colorado River.

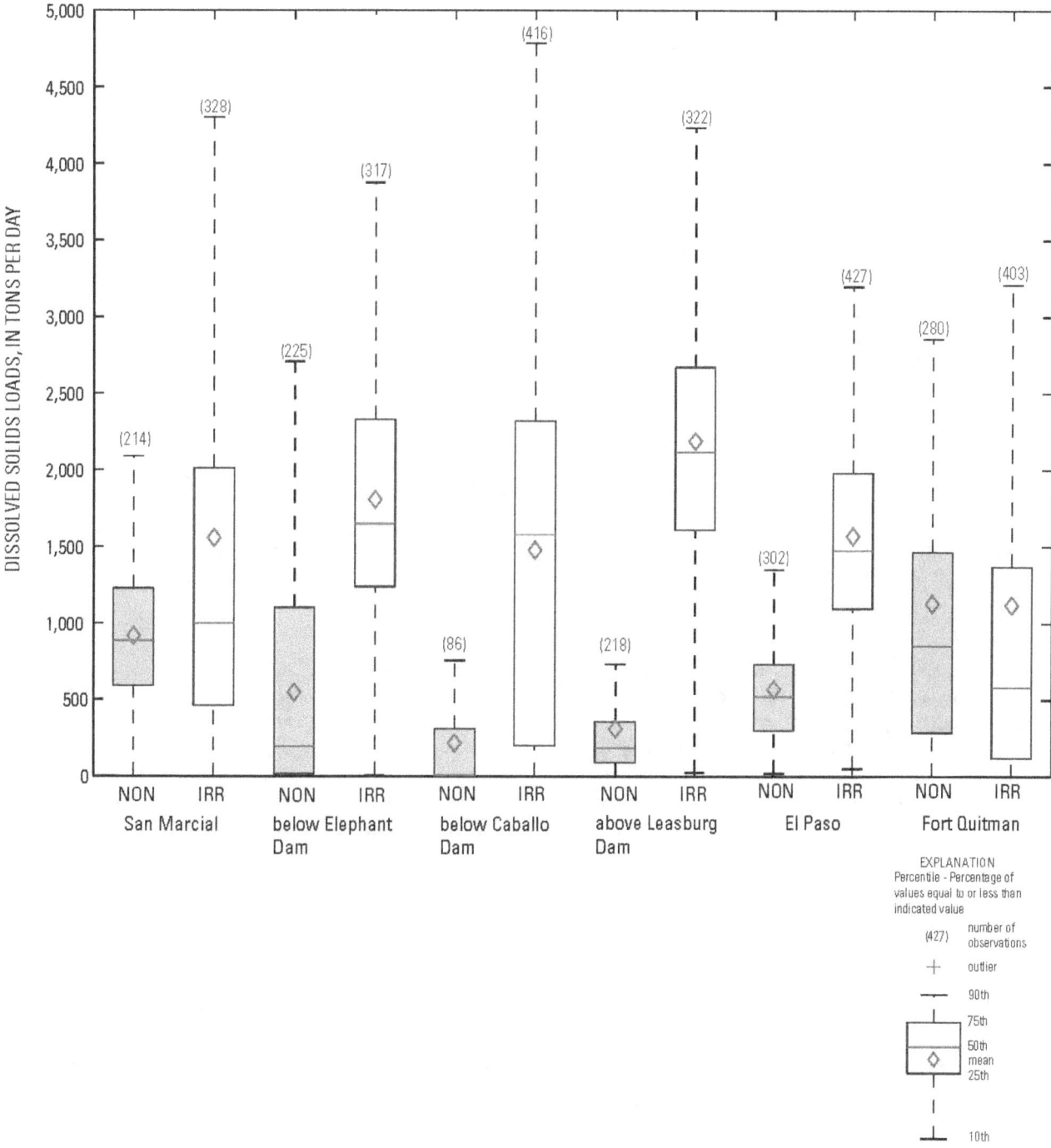

Figure 15. Boxplot of dissolved-solids annual mean loads during the nonirrigation (NON) and irrigation (IRR) season at selected sites in the Rio Grande study area from 1934 to 1999 (Wilcox, 1968; Williams, 2001).

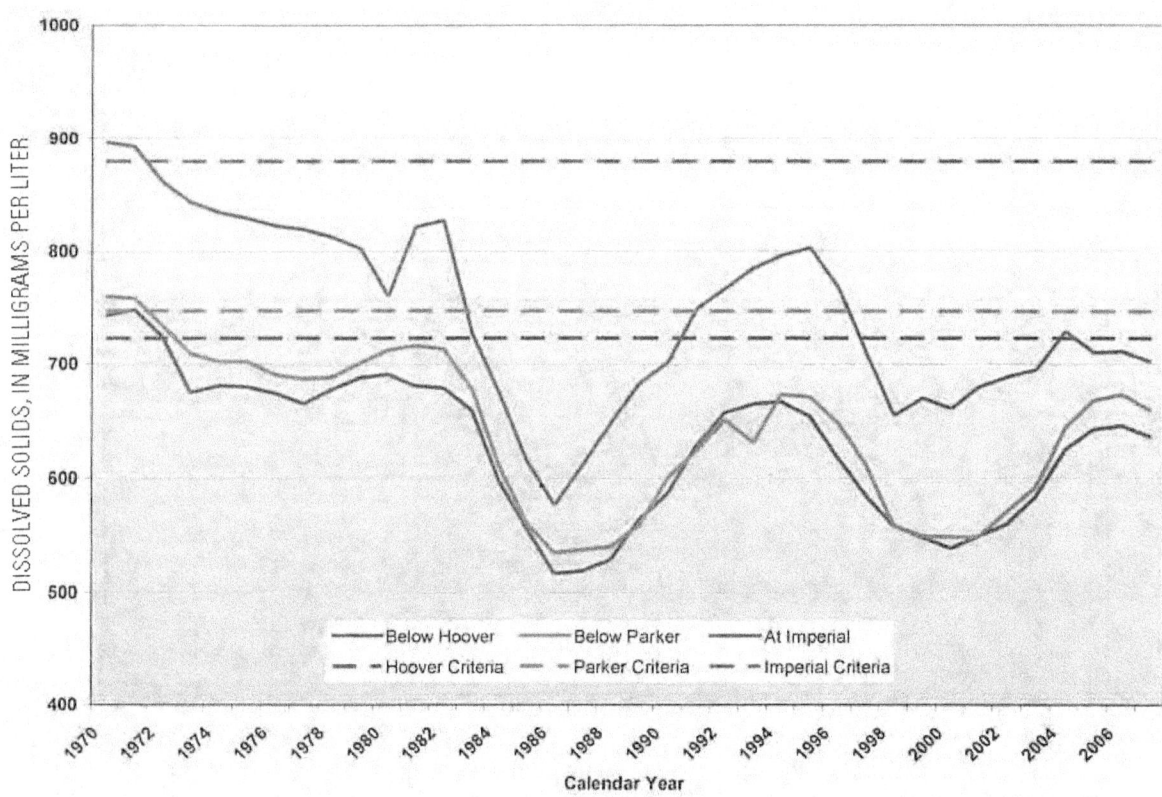

Figure 16. Time series for annual flow-weighted dissolved-solids (TDS) concentration, in milligrams per liter (mg/L), and associated water-quality criteria at three monitoring stations along the Colorado River (from Colorado River Basin Salinity Control Forum, 2008).

Flow-weighted concentrations of dissolved solids at Rio Grande stations monitored by Wilcox (1968) from 1934 to 1963 show a pattern of increasing concentration as the Rio Grande passes from San Marcial to Fort Quitman (fig. 17). The annual median flow-weighted concentrations of dissolved solids in the Rio Grande are as follows: San Marcial, 507 mg/L; Caballo, 504 mg/L; Leasburg, 559 mg/L; El Paso, 731 mg/L; and Fort Quitman, 2,105 mg/L. Data collected by Wilcox (1968) could be used to establish initial water-quality criteria for monitoring stations along the Rio Grande in the study area. However, data collection and the calculation of annual dissolved-solids loads would have to be reinstituted in order to evaluate current conditions for flow-weighted concentrations and to evaluate progress toward dissolved-solids reduction goals.

Data Gaps: Dissolved-Solids Concentrations and Loads

The primary data gaps associated with dissolved-solids concentration and loads are the availability of observed dissolved-solids concentration data, the comparability of loads data, and accuracy and completeness of streamflow data. Following the data-collection effort that occurred between

1934 and 1963 (Wilcox, 1968), extensive gaps in observed water-quality data have occurred (Williams, 2001; Mills, 2003; Lacey, 2006; Bastien, 2009). Large amounts of water-quality data were collected from the Rio Grande at San Acacia, San Marcial, below Elephant Butte Dam, below Caballo Dam, above Leasburg Dam, El Paso, and Fort Quitman from 1934 to 1963. During this period, several water-quality constituents, including dissolved solids and major cations and anions, were monitored. These data allowed the computation of dissolved-solids loads and the identification of spatial and temporal trends in water-quality conditions along the Rio Grande. Since 1963, water-quality data have been collected only sporadically. Water-quality data collected since 1963 have not been collected frequently enough to allow for detailed computations of dissolved-solids loads. The extensive gaps in water-quality data and inconsistency in data available from site to site limit the ability to evaluate long-term changes in water-quality conditions and the ability of water-resource managers to make informed decisions based on current water-quality conditions.

Spatial gaps in the availability of dissolved-solids concentration and load is most evident for the many irrigation drains that transport dissolved solids to the Rio Grande. The drains play an important role in transporting intercepted shallow groundwater and infiltrating irrigation water and associated dissolved solids to the Rio Grande. Dissolved

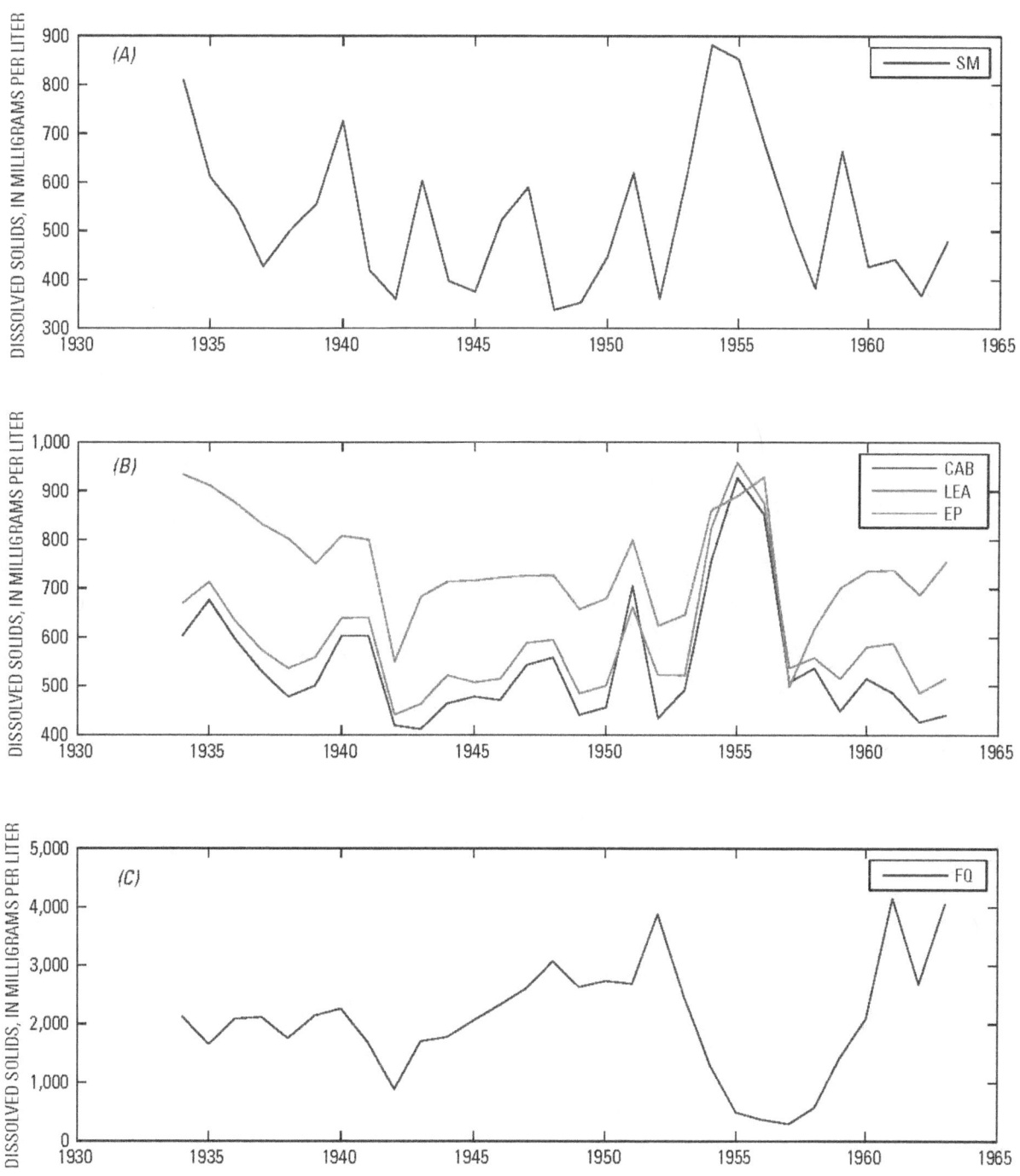

Figure 17.   Time series for annual flow-weighted concentration of dissolved solids in the Rio Grande (*A*) at San Marcial, (*B*) below Caballo Dam and above Leasburg Dam at El Paso, and (*C*) at Fort Quitman for the period 1934–63.

solids are monitored in many of the irrigation drains within the study area; however, the infrequency of data collection in these drains and the absence of water-quality data in others prevent the computation of the dissolved-solids loads being transported by these drains. The absence of dissolved-solids load data for the irrigation drains is a major data gap that limits the understanding of dissolved-solids transport within the Rio Grande study area.

The comparability of calculated loads is another data gap that exists in the current literature. Several studies have calculated loads to address questions related to the transport and mass balance of dissolved solids along the Rio Grande. Various methods and time steps have been used for the computation of dissolved-solids loads. Wilcox (1968) multiplied the total monthly streamflow by the monthly average concentration of dissolved solids to calculate loads. Moore and Anderholm (2002) used multiple linear-regression techniques to compute monthly and annual loads. Mills (2003) calculated instantaneous loads at multiple stations along the continuum of the Rio Grande during winter and summer flow regimes. The question remains, with multiple techniques being employed to describe the downstream flux of dissolved solids, are the resulting loads fully comparable?

Dissolved-Solids Budgets

The ability to account for the mass of dissolved solids transported along the Rio Grande is essential for both researchers who seek to understand the sources and sinks of dissolved solids and for managers who strive to preserve the quality of terrestrial and water resources within the Rio Grande Basin. Two types of budgets for dissolved-solids transport in the Rio Grande have been developed since the early 1900s. The first type of budget defines the relation between the mass of dissolved solids transported, typically monthly or annually, by the Rio Grande into a specified reach to the mass of dissolved solids transported out of the specified reach. If the mass of dissolved solids entering a particular reach of the Rio Grande exceeds the mass of dissolved solids exiting the reach, the mass balance for dissolved solids is considered adverse because dissolved solids are being stored in the agricultural soils or in the shallow alluvial aquifer rather than being transported farther downstream (Wilcox, 1957; Williams, 2001). The first type of dissolved-solids budget is referred to as a basic budget because it defines the balance between the mass of dissolved solids in river inflow and outflow for a defined reach of the Rio Grande. The second type of budget, referred to as a complex budget, accounts for all sources (such as, tributaries, agricultural drains, municipal wastewater effluent, mineral dissolution, and groundwater discharge) and sinks (such as, irrigation diversions, municipal diversions, groundwater recharge, and mineral precipitation) of dissolved solids such that the mass balance between the inflows to and outflows from a specified reach of the Rio

Grande equals zero. The development of complex budgets has been made more possible during the past decade because newly developed hydrogeological, geophysical, and hydrochemical analyses allow for the quantitative identification of significant contributing sources (Mills, 2003; Phillips and others, 2003; Hogan and others, 2007; Eastoe and others, 2007; Moore and others, 2008).

Basic Budgets

Basic budgets, which describe whether dissolved solids are being stored or released from a specified reach in the Rio Grande in the study area, have been developed and described by Williams (2001) and Witcher and others (2004). Williams (2001) described the balance between the mass of dissolved solids in river inflow and outflow for the following reaches of the Rio Grande: (1) San Marcial to below Elephant Butte Dam, (2) below Elephant Butte Dam to below Caballo Dam, (3) below Caballo Dam to above Leasburg Dam, (4) above Leasburg Dam to El Paso (Courchesne Bridge), and (5) El Paso to Fort Quitman. The mass balance for the dissolved solids transported monthly in river inflow and outflow for each reach was determined by subtracting total monthly outflow from the total monthly inflow. If the inflow of dissolved solids is less than the outflow (negative values), the mass balance of dissolved solids generally is considered beneficial because dissolved solids are being released rather than stored or accumulated in the specified reach (Wilcox, 1957; Williams, 2001; Witcher and others, 2004). A negative mass balance for dissolved solids can be a result of inflow of dissolved solids from tributaries, municipal wastewater effluent, mineral dissolution, and(or) groundwater discharge that occurs along the length of the specified reach. Conversely, if the inflow of dissolved solids is greater than the outflow (positive values), the mass balance of dissolved solids is considered adverse because dissolved solids are being stored in rather than released from the specified reach (Wilcox, 1957; Williams, 2001; Witcher and others, 2004). Dissolved solids can be stored through many transport and storage processes that include leakage of surface water and groundwater to the groundwater system, mineral precipitation, ion exchange, reservoir storage, and surface-water and groundwater withdrawals. The concern associated with the storage of dissolved solids is that their accumulation can lead to the degradation of agricultural soils and(or) groundwater resources.

The cumulative mass balances of dissolved solids for reaches along the Rio Grande in the study area, as described by Williams (2001) and Witcher and others (2004), are presented in figure 18. The cumulative mass balance for the reach from San Marcial to below Elephant Butte Dam shows that dissolved solids over the entire period were being stored; however, the temporal variation in the cumulative mass balance shows that the balance trends positive during high-flow periods and trends negative during low-flow periods

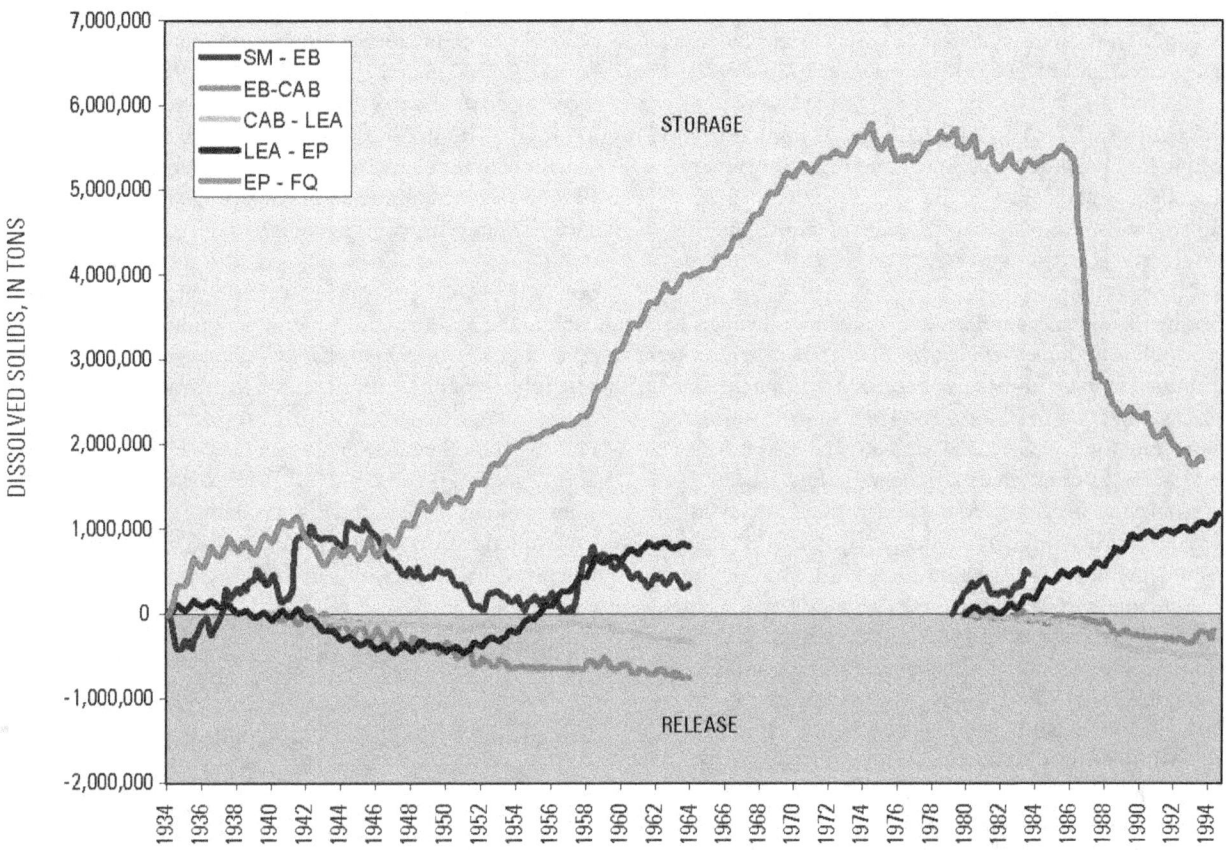

Figure 18. Cumulative mass balance for dissolved solids transported monthly in specified reaches along the Rio Grande study area (from Williams, 2001; used with permission). Specified reaches include San Marcial to below Elephant Butte Dam (SM – EB), below Elephant Butte Dam to below Caballo Dam (EB – CAB), below Caballo Dam to above Leasburg Dam (CAB – LEA), above Leasburg Dam to El Paso (Courchesne Bridge; LEA – EP), and El Paso to Fort Quitman (EP – FQ).

(Williams, 2001) and is driven in large part by changes in storage in Elephant Butte Reservoir (Lacey, 2006). Witcher and others (2004) suggest that this temporal variation is a result of water and solutes being stored in Elephant Butte Reservoir during high-flow periods and subsequently released during low-flow periods. Other possibilities for the overall positive trend in mass balance are groundwater recharge and(or) mineral precipitation in the reservoir (Witcher and others, 2004).

The cumulative mass balance for the reach below Elephant Butte Dam to below Caballo Dam indicates dissolved solids were being released, approximately 700,000 tons during 1934–63 (fig. 18; Witcher and others, 2004). The negative mass balance for dissolved solids are attributed to tributary discharge to Caballo Reservoir during storm-runoff events or, more importantly, the discharge of saline groundwater of geothermal origin to the Rio Grande at Truth or Consequences, New Mexico (Cox and Reeder, 1962; Witcher and others, 2004).

The cumulative mass balance for the reach from below Caballo Dam to above Leasburg Dam shows that dissolved solids were being released from this reach, approximately 300,000 tons (fig. 18; Witcher and others, 2004). Witcher and others (2004) attribute this negative salt balance to mineral dissolution in the soils of the Rincon Valley. In addition to mineral dissolution, Anderholm (2002) suggests that discharge of regional groundwater contributes to the high dissolved-solids concentration in the region of the Rincon Drain and at the distal end of the Palomas Basin.

The cumulative mass balance for the reach from above Leasburg Dam to El Paso indicates considerable variability. The dissolved-solids balance for this reach was primarily negative (released dissolved solids) for the period 1934–51; however, the drought that occurred during the 1950s reversed the dissolved-solids balance to a primarily positive one (stored dissolved solids; fig. 18). Approximately 700,000 tons of dissolved solids were stored in this reach during 1955–63, and 1,500,000 tons were stored during 1979–94.

The cumulative mass balance for the reach from El Paso to Fort Quitman shows that dissolved solids primarily were stored, approximately 5,500,000 tons during 1934–75 (fig. 18; Witcher and others, 2004). The reversal of the cumulative mass-balance trend from positive to negative starting in 1986 has been linked to spillway overflow and high-flow releases from Elephant Butte Reservoir that subsequently flushed accumulated salts, equivalent to 30 years of storage, in this reach of the river (Miyamoto and others, 1995; Witcher and others, 2004).

The results of the cumulative mass-balance analysis for dissolved solids (Witcher and others, 2004) indicate long-term and continued storage of dissolved solids in the reaches from above Leasburg Dam to El Paso and from El Paso to Fort Quitman along the Rio Grande. One potential explanation for the increased storage in these reaches is loss of water and solutes from the Rio Grande to the underlying alluvial aquifer. West (1995) discussed the influences of the 1950s drought and increased dependence on groundwater supplies in the Mesilla Basin on streamflow. Increased groundwater diversions in the Mesilla Basin have reduced flow in the irrigation drains, thus reducing the amount of salts being flushed from the alluvial aquifer. Hibbs and Boghici (1999) also showed that the El Paso-Ciudad Juarez reach of the Rio Grande is a losing reach during all flow conditions, and the loss has been intensified since the 1970s as a result of groundwater pumping for municipal water supply. Wilson and others (1981) described the dissolved solids in the alluvial aquifer beneath the Mesilla Basin as having three unique zones—upper, middle, and lower—based on the associated concentration of dissolved solids. The upper zone generally has dissolved-solids concentrations ranging from 1,000 to 3,000 mg/L. The middle zone generally has dissolved-solids concentrations that are less than 500 mg/L. The lower zone generally has dissolved-solids concentrations that are greater than 3,000 mg/L. The large dissolved-solids concentrations in the upper zone of the alluvial aquifer beneath the Mesilla Basin may be a result of groundwater recharge from the Rio Grande and irrigation systems and concentration of these irrigation waters (Wilson and others, 1981; Witcher and others, 2004). Walton and others (1999) described that, in the Mesilla Basin, (1) irrigation and associated evaporation leads to increased dissolved-solids concentrations in the shallow alluvial aquifer; (2) the large dissolved-solids concentrations overlie the lower dissolved-solids concentrations in the intermediate depths; and (3) groundwater pumping for irrigation draws water with large dissolved-solids concentration water into the lower-concentration water of the intermediate depths.

There also is variation in the cumulative mass balances for the individual major ions, both temporally and spatially (Witcher and others, 2004). For example, the cumulative mass balance for major ions transported in the Rio Grande between Leasburg Dam and El Paso indicate two general patterns (fig. 19). Calcium, magnesium, sulfate, and bicarbonate all exhibit positive cumulative mass balance for the period 1934–63 and 1980–94 (fig. 19). Conversely, sodium and chloride exhibit negative cumulative mass balance for the periods 1934–63 and 1980–94 (fig. 19); that is, more of these ions are leaving the basin at El Paso than entering at Leasburg. The storage of calcium, magnesium, sulfate, and bicarbonate in the reaches from Leasburg to El Paso and from El Paso to Fort Quitman can be attributed to the diversion of surface water for irrigation combined with a reduction in the drain flows (compounded by groundwater pumping), which otherwise would have transported irrigation return flows back to the Rio Grande, mineral precipitation, groundwater pumping, and(or) ion exchange (Witcher and others, 2004). The release of chloride along the Rio Grande has been investigated extensively during the past decade (Mills, 2003; Phillips and others, 2003; Lacey, 2006; Hibbs and Merino, 2007; Hogan and others, 2007; Moore and others, 2008). These studies have found that discharge of saline groundwater (rich in chloride and sodium) to the Rio Grande is the primary source of dissolved solids in the Rio Grande study area.

Complex Budgets

The goal for the development of complex solute budgets is to quantitatively represent all solute inflows and outflows such that the solute balance equals zero. Recent studies in the Rio Grande study area have focused on the development of complex budgets for solutes (Mills, 2003; Lacey, 2006; Bastien, 2009). The majority of the research focus was on developing complex budgets for chloride (Mills, 2003; Lacey, 2006). Chloride was chosen because it is a conservative constituent that is not involved in chemical reactions with the surrounding environment. Results from these chloride-based investigations indicate that the dominant source contributing chloride to the Rio Grande is the discharge of saline groundwater to the Rio Grande; this discharge occurs primarily at the distal end of each alluvial-fill basin (Mills, 2003; Phillips and others, 2003; Lacey, 2006; Hibbs and Merino, 2007; Hogan and others, 2007; Moore and others, 2008). However, based on the cumulative mass-balance analysis for dissolved solids and major ions (Williams, 2001; Witcher and others, 2004), using complex budgets for chloride alone to describe the inflows and outflows of dissolved solids to the Rio Grande in the study area may not be completely representative.

Mills (2003) developed complex budgets that represent chloride transport during both the irrigation (figs. 20, 21) and nonirrigation seasons (figs. 22, 23). These budgets represent the mass of chloride that is transported into and out of the Rio Grande from the headwaters in Colorado to Fort Quitman, Texas, during two snapshots in time – August 2001 and January 2002. The structure of the pipe diagrams that represent chloride transport (figs. 20–23) shows (1) the flux of chloride being delivered by the Rio Grande in blue; (2) the inflows (gains) of chloride to the Rio Grande (tributaries, wastewater-treatment plants, agricultural drains,

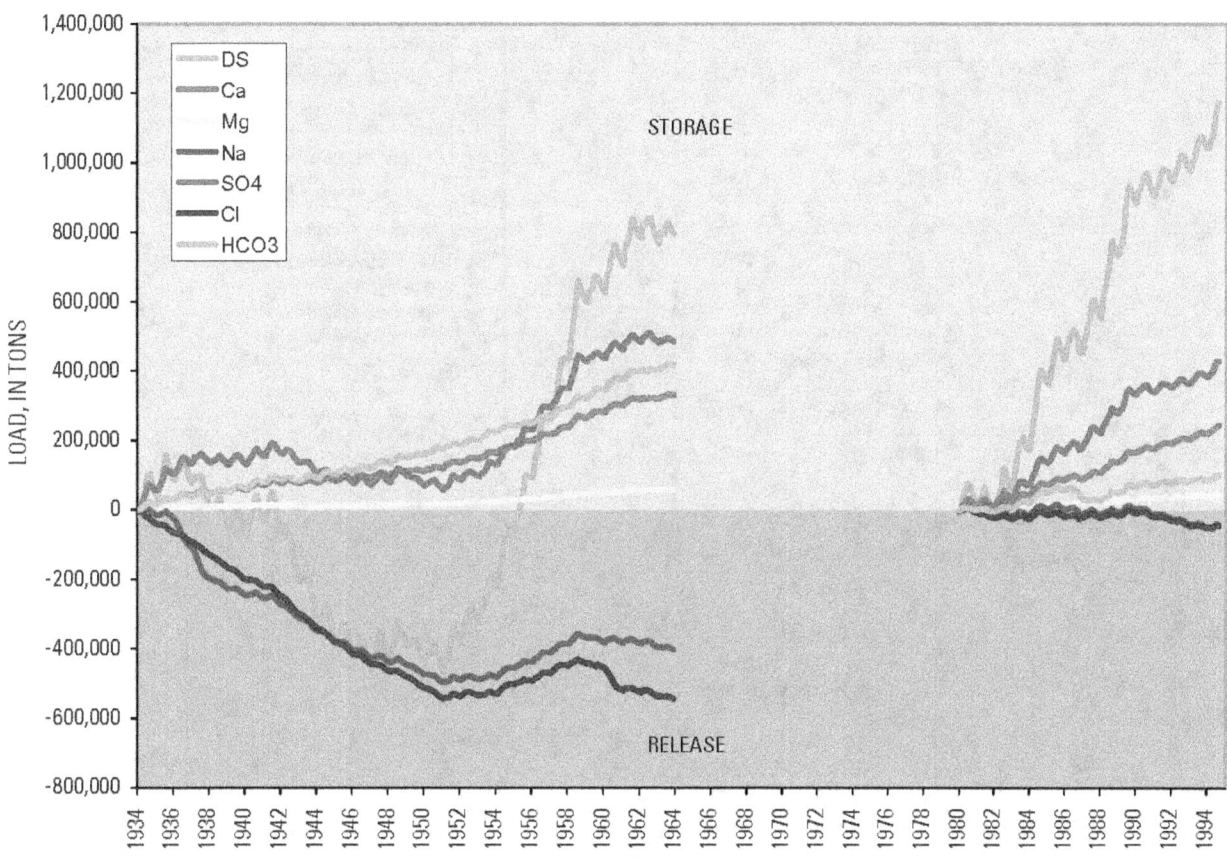

Figure 19. Cumulative mass balance for dissolved solids (DS), calcium (Ca), magnesium (Mg), sodium (Na), sulfate (SO4), chloride (Cl), and bicarbonate (HCO3) transported monthly in the reach of the Rio Grande above Leasburg Dam to El Paso (from Williams, 2001; used with permission).

and groundwater seepage), which are represented on the left side of the pipe diagram; and (3) the outflows (losses) of chloride from the Rio Grande (irrigation diversions and seepage), which are represented on the right side of the pipe diagram. The flux of chloride for each source represented on the pipe diagram is based on (1) chloride concentration from a single water-quality sample and stream discharge obtained from the associated gaging stations; or (2) estimated chloride concentration and discharge based on previously published values. The pipe diagram for August 2001 (irrigation season) reveals that the chloride flux increases considerably below Elephant Butte Dam as a result of water and associated chloride released from Elephant Butte Reservoir (figs. 20, 21). The flux of chloride leaving the Rio Grande (irrigation diversions and seepage) far exceeds the flux of chloride entering the Rio Grande. The flux of chloride in the Rio Grande below Elephant Butte Reservoir during the irrigation season is nearly completely removed by irrigation diversions by the time the Rio Grande reaches the El Paso-Hudspeth County line (river distance about 1,021 km from the

headwaters). The flux then increases to levels greater than what were released originally from Elephant Butte Reservoir in the Rio Grande between the El Paso-Hudspeth County line and Fort Quitman, Texas (fig. 21). The pipe diagram for January 2002 (nonirrigation season) shows that the flux of chloride in the Rio Grande is diminished considerably compared to August 2001, which is a result of water and chloride being stored in Elephant Butte Reservoir (figs. 22, 23). The chloride flux in the Rio Grande markedly increases near San Acacia (about 660 km from the headwaters), which is the area where the Rio Grande moves from the Albuquerque Basin to the Socorro Basin (fig. 22). The chloride flux is reduced considerably in the Rio Grande below Caballo Dam, but it steadily increases to the El Paso-Hudspeth County line and markedly increases between the El Paso-Hudspeth County line and Fort Quitman (fig. 23). Increases in the flux of chloride in the Rio Grande during January 2002 were attributed to the inflow of chloride from saline groundwater, agricultural drains, and wastewater-treatment plants (Mills, 2003).

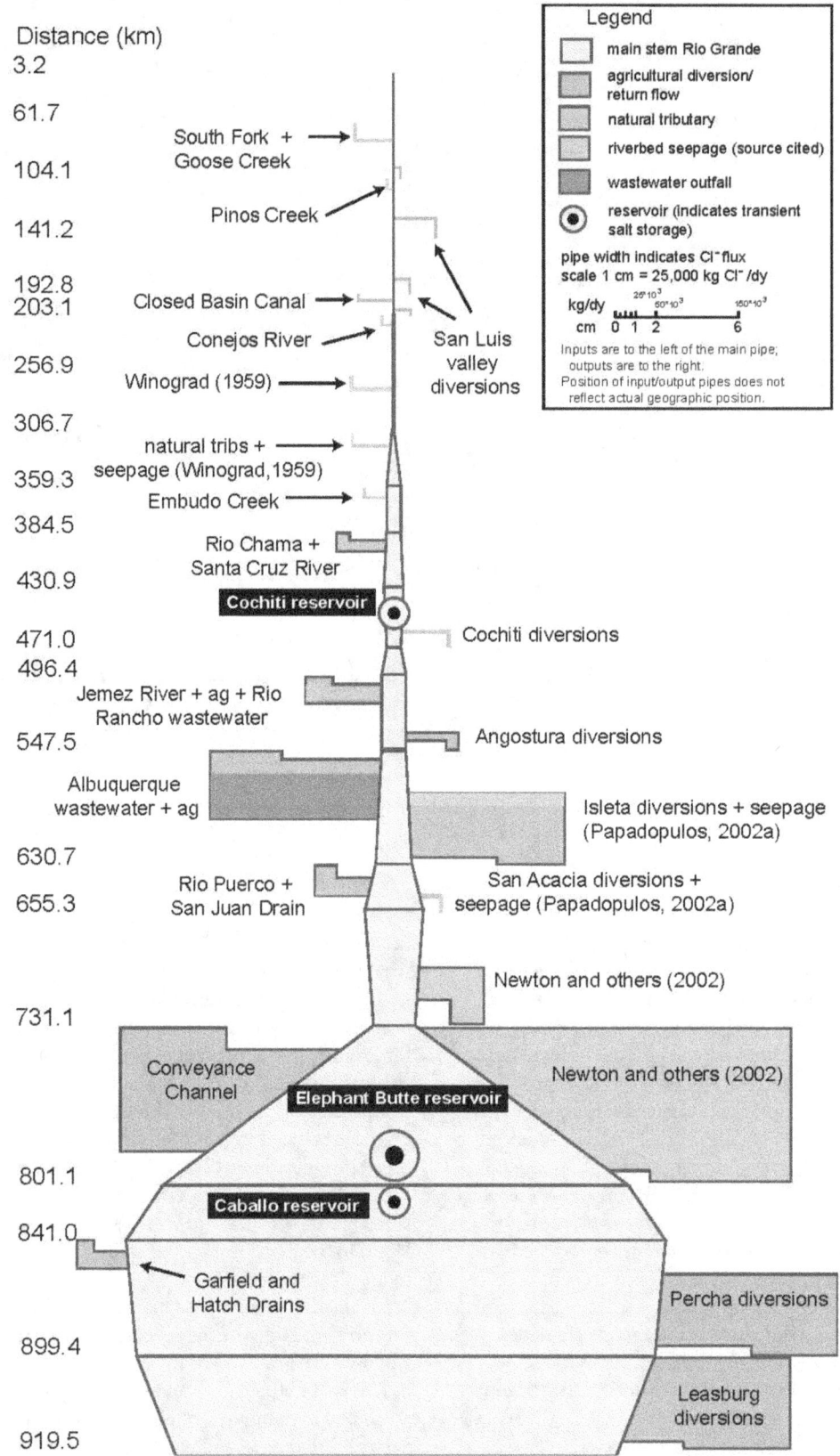

Figure 20.   Pipe diagram of chloride burden of the Rio Grande, its modeled tributaries and diversions, August 2001 (kilograms per day; kg/d). River distance 3.2–919.5 kilometers (km) (figure from Mills, 2003; used with permission).

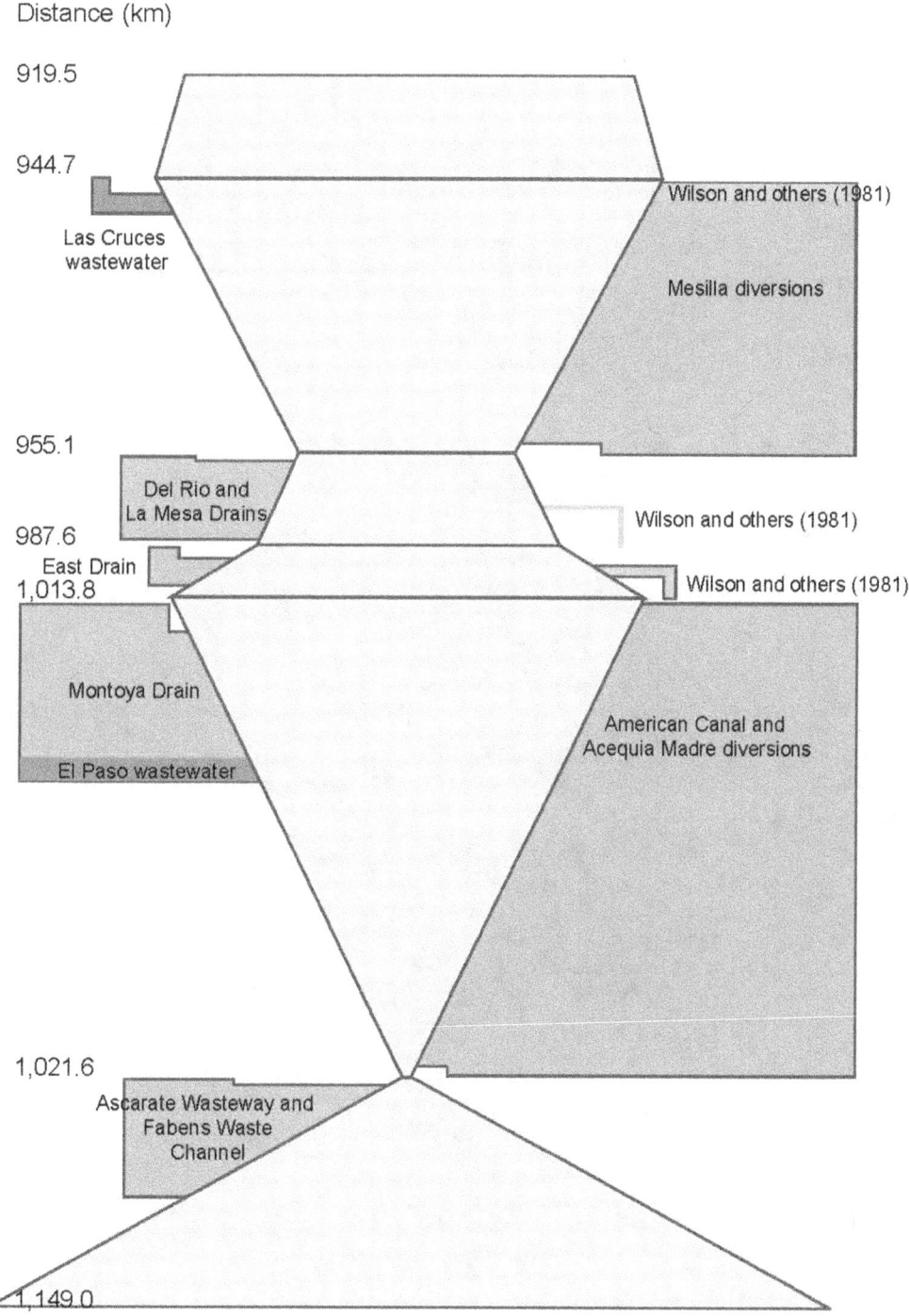

Distance (km)

919.5

944.7

Las Cruces
wastewater

Wilson and others (1981)

Mesilla diversions

955.1

Del Rio and
La Mesa Drains

Wilson and others (1981)

987.6

East Drain

1,013.8

Wilson and others (1981)

Montoya Drain

American Canal and
Acequia Madre diversions

El Paso wastewater

1,021.6

Ascarate Wasteway and
Fabens Waste
Channel

1,149.0

Figure 21.   Pipe diagram of chloride burden of the Rio Grande, its modeled tributaries and diversions, August 2001 (kilograms per day; kg/d). River distance 919.5–1,149.0 kilometers (km) (figure from Mills, 2003; used with permission).

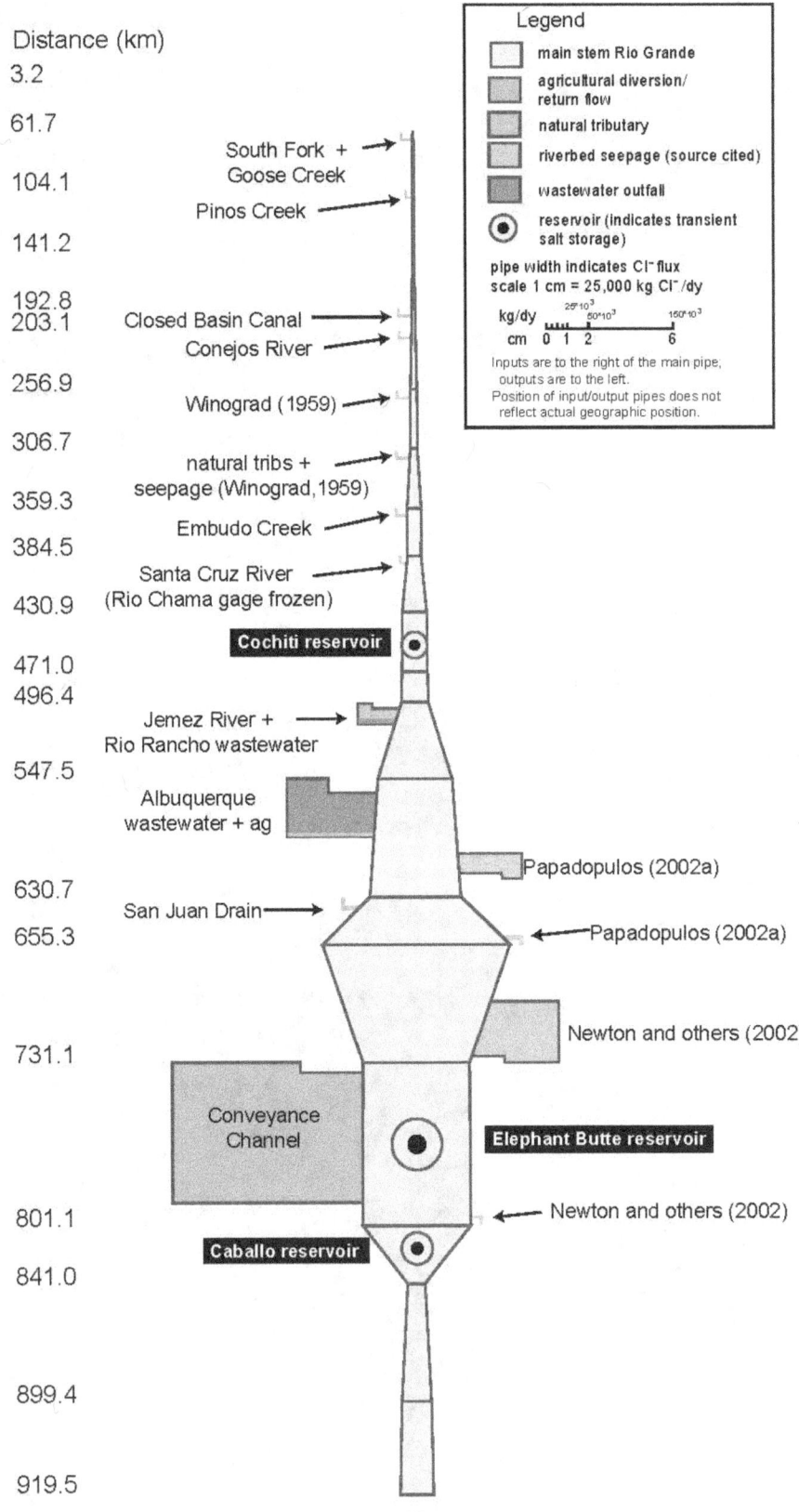

Figure 22.   Pipe diagram of chloride burden of the Rio Grande, its modeled tributaries and diversions, January 2002 (kilograms per day; kg/d). River distance 3.2–919.5 kilometers (km) (figure from Mills, 2003; used with permission).

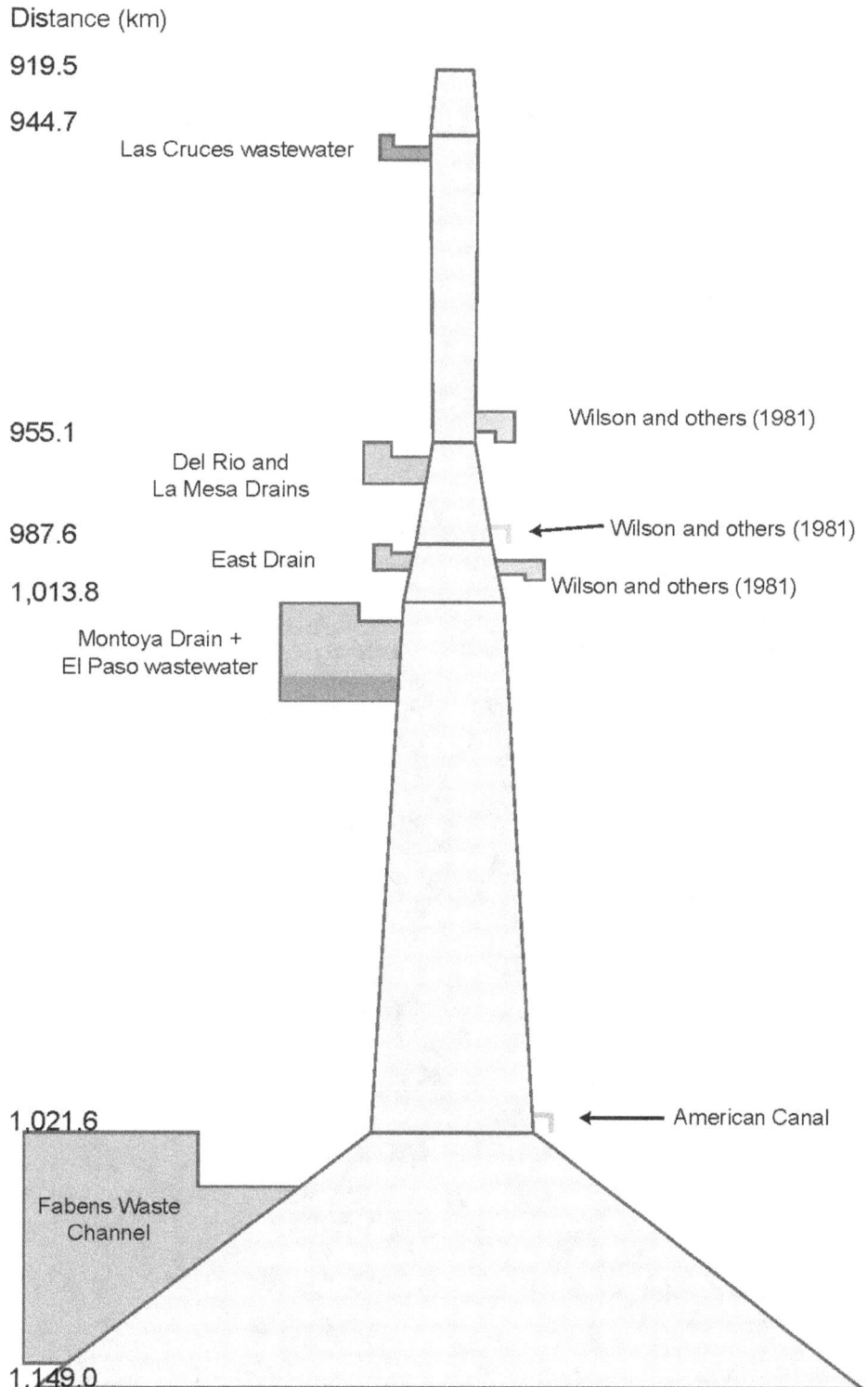

Distance (km)

919.5

944.7
Las Cruces wastewater

955.1
Del Rio and
La Mesa Drains

Wilson and others (1981)

987.6
East Drain

Wilson and others (1981)

Wilson and others (1981)

1,013.8
Montoya Drain +
El Paso wastewater

1,021.6
Fabens Waste
Channel

American Canal

1,149.0

Figure 23.   Pipe diagram of chloride burden of the Rio Grande, its modeled tributaries and diversions, January 2002 (kilograms per day; kg/d). River distance 919.5–1,149.0 kilometers (km) (figure from Mills, 2003; used with permission).

Mills (2003) computed the cumulative influence that each chloride source, identified during the August 2001 sampling event, had on the associated total chloride load in the Rio Grande (fig. 24). The inflow of chloride from deep groundwater accounted for 37 percent of the total chloride load. The majority of the chloride delivered by deep groundwater occurred in the Rio Grande between Elephant Butte Reservoir and El Paso (approximately 770 to 1,000 km). The inflow of chloride from natural tributaries and wastewater-treatment plants accounted for 28 and 26 percent of the chloride load in the Rio Grande, respectively. Finally, 9 percent of the total chloride load in the Rio Grande was attributed to processes that occur within Elephant Butte Reservoir. The chloride contribution attributed to Elephant Butte Reservoir was defined as the difference between the inflow of chloride to Elephant Butte Reservoir and the amount of chloride discharged from Elephant Butte Dam.

Chloride-flux information produced by Mills (2003) provides a detailed picture of the magnitude of fluxes of chloride entering and leaving the Rio Grande. The pipe diagrams for chloride flux clearly show where chloride is entering and leaving the Rio Grande; however, caution should be used when interpreting these figures. First, the chloride-flux information presented by Mills (2003; figs. 20–23) are based on two snapshots in time (August 2001 and January 2002) and probably do not reflect the variability inherent in the various long-term transport and storage processes. Second, many of the inflows and outflows of chloride are estimated based on values obtained from the literature and not directly measured. Finally, the pipe diagrams provide a detailed picture of chloride fluxes but do not account for the inflow and outflow of other dominant constituents contributing to the dissolved solids in the Rio Grande, such as sodium, calcium, sulfate, and bicarbonate.

Bastien (2009) developed complex budgets for dissolved solids and major ions for selected reaches in the Rio Grande study area between San Acacia and El Paso. The reaches of the Rio Grande that were included in the complex budget development are (1) San Acacia to San Marcial, (2) San Marcial to below Elephant Butte Dam, (3) below Elephant Butte Dam to below Caballo Dam, and (4) below Caballo Dam to El Paso (Courchesne Bridge). Bastien (2009) chose to develop complex budgets for dissolved solids as an average load for decadal time periods: 1930–39, 1940–49, 1950–59, 1960–69, 1970–79, 1980–89, and 1990–99, given that the relation between inflow and outflows of dissolved solids varies temporally. Bastien (2009) represented three sources of dissolved solids to each reach of the Rio Grande: (1) Rio Grande inflow, (2) groundwater discharge to Rio Grande, and (3) brine. Rio Grande inflow represents the mass of dissolved solids that were transported by the Rio Grande into each specified reach in the study area. Much of the Rio Grande inflow data were obtained from Wilcox (1968) and Williams (2001). Groundwater discharge represents the mass of dissolved solids that are transported to the Rio Grande from the underlying alluvial aquifer. Data for groundwater discharge were based on published seepage studies for the volume of discharge and on Plummer and others (2004) for the quality of the discharge. Brine represents the discharge of saline groundwater to the Rio Grande. Data for the contribution of brines within each reach were based on published discharge and water-quality data from Newton (2005) and Moore and others (2008). Additionally, Bastien (2009) represents a category called "Rio Grande Inflow+," which is the sum of the Rio Grande inflow, groundwater seepage, and brine categories. The "Rio Grande Inflow+" is the estimated amount of dissolved solids that would leave a given reach if the balance equaled zero. The actual outflow from each reach is represented by the "Rio Grande Outflow" category.

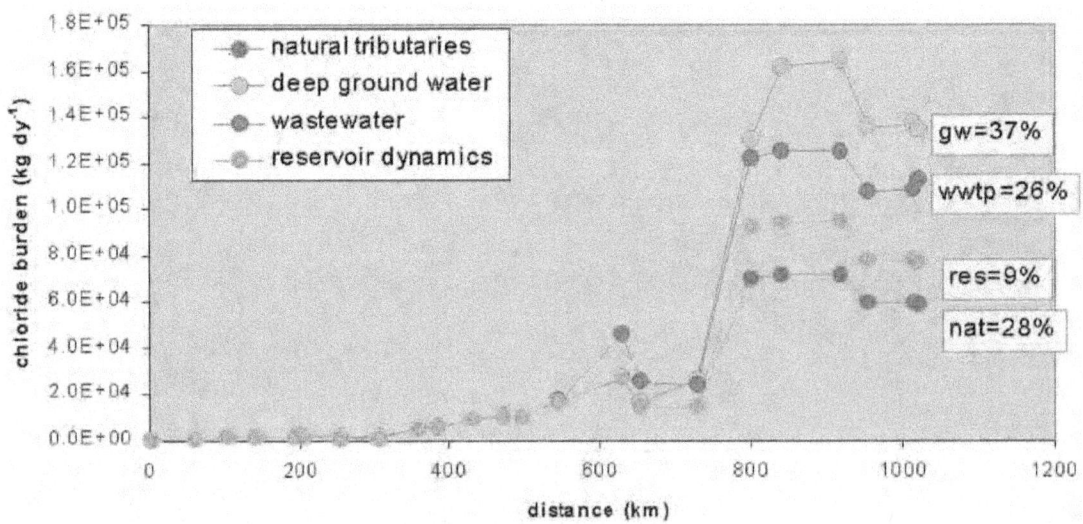

Figure 24.   Stacked graph of cumulative chloride addition by natural tributaries (nat), wastewater effluent (wwtp), deep groundwater (gw), and Elephant Butte Reservoir (res) dynamics, August 2001 (figure from Mills, 2003; used with permission).

Results from the complex budget development by Bastien (2009) are presented in table 1. As part of the evaluation of each complex budget for dissolved solids, the estimated inflow of dissolved solids (Rio Grande Inflow+) was compared to the measured outflow (Rio Grande Outflow). Discrepancies between the estimated inflow and measured outflow were attributed to chemical interactions with mineral phases, including aluminosilicate weathering reactions, dedolomitization, dissolution of minerals, and ion exchange interactions; each chemical interaction may act as a source or a sink for dissolved solids in irrigated or riparian areas (Bastien, 2009). The discrepancy between estimated inflow and measured outflow also could be attributed to groundwater and surface-water interactions and subsequent storage of dissolved solids in the underlying alluvial aquifer. Bastien (2009) concluded that dissolved-solids loads in the Rio Grande study area are controlled by three mechanisms. These mechanisms are groundwater seepage (discharge to Rio Grande), direct discharge of saline groundwater, and mineral interactions.

A budget for dissolved solids in the Rio Grande between El Paso and Fort Quitman was presented by Miyamoto and others (1995). The major inflows of dissolved solids in this reach of the Rio Grande were represented as Rio Grande inflow at El Paso and municipal wastewater effluent from El Paso (table 2). The major outflows for dissolved solids were represented as those dissolved solids lost through diversions to the American and Mexican Canals as well as Rio Grande outflow at Fort Quitman (table 2). The mass-balance analysis for dissolved solids indicated that, on average, 64,000 tons were accumulated annually in the reach from El Paso to Fort Quitman reach during 1969–89. The mass-balance result from Miyamoto and others (1995) is in agreement with the results from Williams (2001) and Witcher and others (2004), who showed that dissolved solids are being stored rather than released from this reach.

Summary of Dissolved-Solids Budgets

Results from existing basic and complex budgets for dissolved solids in the Rio Grande provide valuable information pertaining to the mass of dissolved solids that is transported and(or) stored in designated reaches as well as the dominant sources that deliver dissolved solids to the Rio Grande. Results from basic dissolved-solids budgets for each reach in the Rio Grande study area revealed that three of the five reaches typically store more dissolved solids than are released; these reaches are San Marcial to below Elephant Butte Dam, above Leasburg Dam to El Paso, and El Paso to Fort Quitman. Storage in the reach from San Marcial to below Elephant Butte Dam has been attributed to storage in Elephant Butte Reservoir and the associated shallow alluvial aquifer. Storage in the reaches from above Leasburg Dam to El Paso and El Paso to Fort Quitman has been attributed

to groundwater recharge, surface-water and groundwater withdrawals, and mineral precipitation. The concern regarding storage in theses reaches is the potential for degradation of agricultural soils and(or) groundwater resources through increased salinization. The remaining two reaches, which are below Elephant Butte Dam to below Caballo Dam and below Caballo Dam to above Leasburg Dam, transport more dissolved solids out of each respective reach than what entered each reach. This increase in dissolved solids in these two reaches has been attributed primarily to the inflow of saline groundwater near Truth or Consequences, New Mexico, and at the distal end of the Palomas Basin. Results from complex budgets indicate that the primary sources of dissolved solids entering the Rio Grande are derived from the inflow of saline groundwater, inflow of regional groundwater, and chemical reactions between mineral phases. The implication of these results for water-resource managers attempting to mitigate salinization along the Rio Grande is that they will have to consider both the inflow of saline and regional groundwater to the Rio Grande and the water and dissolved solids from the Rio Grande that are stored in agricultural soils and the shallow alluvial aquifer.

Data Gaps: Dissolved-Solids Budgets

The computation of detailed budgets for the transport of dissolved solids and associated water-quality constituents is essential for the management of the Rio Grande water resources. Advancements in geochemical and isotopic analyses have enabled researchers to determine that most of the dissolved solids in the Rio Grande are derived from groundwater sources, such as discharge of saline groundwater derived from geothermal and nongeothermal sources. However, the ability for researchers to accurately quantify the flux of dissolved solids from the various groundwater-derived sources currently is not possible. The values represented in the previously discussed complex budgets that describe the contribution of saline groundwater to the Rio Grande are derived from published values for general discharge rates and water-quality. Accurate and reach-specific computations for the load of dissolved solids derived from the various groundwater sources are essential for future dissolved-solids mitigation efforts.

Another data gap associated with the development and representation of complex budgets for specified reaches along the Rio Grande in the study area is the lack of direct measurement, or quantification, of the amount of dissolved solids stored in the underlying alluvial aquifer or associated soils. Bastien (2009) discusses the losses of dissolved solids through chemical and mineral interactions. However, the presentation of detailed budgets to date show inflow fluxes of dissolved solids or chloride and do not show the outflow fluxes (losses) from the Rio Grande to the underlying alluvial aquifer.

Table 1.   Mass balance for the monthly average dissolved solids transported in the Rio Grande between (1) San Acacia to San Marcial (SA to SM), (2) San Marcial to below Elephant Butte Dam (SM to EB), (3) below Elephant Butte Dam to below Caballo Dam (EB to CAB), and (4) below Caballo Dam to El Paso (Courchesne) (CAB to EP) for each decade from 1930–99. Data from Bastien, 2009.

[Rio Grande Inflow+, sum of Rio Grande Inflow, Groundwater Seepage, and Brine Inflow; nd, no data; --, value listed as a zero in Bastien (2009)]

Source	SA to SM (tons per month)	SM to EB (tons per month)	EB to CAB (tons per month)	CAB to EP (tons per month)
1930 to 1939				
Rio Grande inflow	nd	29,785	44,597	nd
Groundwater seepage	404	273	1,011	5,320
Brine inflow	nd	4,161	--	--
Rio Grande inflow+	nd	34,219	45,608	nd
Rio Grande outflow	29,785	44,597	nd	49,687
1940 to 1949				
Rio Grande inflow	47,302	41,288	47,132	51,508
Groundwater seepage	404	273	1,011	5,320
Brine inflow	1,122	3,079	2,364	5,009
Rio Grande inflow+	48,827	44,641	50,507	61,837
Rio Grande outflow	41,288	47,132	51,508	57,945
1950 to 1959				
Rio Grande inflow	nd	41,366	27,998	30,133
Groundwater seepage	404	273	1,011	5,320
Brine inflow	nd	--	1,090	--
Rio Grande inflow+	nd	41,639	30,099	35,453
Rio Grande outflow	41,366	27,998	30,133	21,577
1960 to 1969				
Rio Grande inflow	39,671	54,497	26,772	28,494
Groundwater seepage	404	273	1,011	5,320
Brine inflow	4,983	--	1,198	107
Rio Grande inflow+	45,058	54,770	28,981	33,921
Rio Grande outflow	39,671	54,497	26,772	28,494
1970 to 1979				
Rio Grande inflow	35,358	50,140	21,804	--
Groundwater seepage	404	273	1,011	5,320
Brine inflow	--	--	--	13,381
Rio Grande inflow+	35,762	50,413	22,814	--
Rio Grande outflow	50,140	21,804	--	56,241
1980 to 1989				
Rio Grande inflow	37,433	52,694	39,431	41,539
Groundwater seepage	404	273	1,011	5,320
Brine inflow	3,839	129	2,013	3,687
Rio Grande inflow+	41,676	53,097	42,455	50,546
Rio Grande outflow	52,694	44,777	41,539	53,052
1990 to 1999				
Rio Grande inflow	33,306	44,425	39,851	41,877
Groundwater seepage	404	273	1,011	5,320
Brine inflow	4,385	190	1,762	59
Rio Grande inflow+	38,095	44,888	42,624	47,256
Rio Grande outflow	44,425	39,851	41,877	37,241

Table 2. Mass balance for annual average dissolved solids transported in the Rio Grande between El Paso and Fort Quitman during 1969–89. Data from Miyamoto and others, 1995.

[nd = no data]

Source	Dissolved solids (million tons per year)
Inflows	
Rio Grande inflow – El Paso	0.425
Municipal sewage effluent – El Paso	0.042
Outflows	
American Canal	0
Mexican Canal	0.051
Rio Grande outflow – Fort Quitman	0.352
Balance	
Mass balance (inflow minus outflow)	0.064

Location of Areas with High Concentrations of Dissolved Solids

Many studies have investigated the hydrogeology and associated water-quality conditions along the Rio Grande and underlying alluvial-fill basins. During these investigations, researchers have identified areas of surface water and(or) groundwater that contain unusually high concentrations of dissolved solids or associated water-quality constituents compared to the nearby water-quality conditions (Appendix 2). This section identifies areas that contain high concentrations of dissolved solids and discusses potential sources that contribute to this water-quality condition. These areas have the potential to contribute substantial amounts of dissolved solids to the Rio Grande and need to be considered for future investigations and(or) future locations of dissolved-solids mitigation efforts. The organizing features for this section are the alluvial-fill basins that underlie the Rio Grande from San Acacia, New Mexico, to Fort Quitman, Texas. The locations of areas containing high dissolved-solids concentration will be discussed for the Socorro, San Marcial, Engle, Palomas, Mesilla, and Hueco Basins. Detailed description of the spatial extent and hydrogeology of these alluvial-fill basins can be found in Wilkins (1986).

Socorro Basin

The Socorro Basin underlies the Rio Grande from San Acacia to San Marcial. The hydrogeology and water quality of the Socorro Basin was extensively studied by Anderholm (1987). During this investigation, Anderholm (1987) identified two distinct regions of the Socorro Basin that have values of specific conductance and chloride concentrations that are larger than those in surrounding areas (Appendix 2; fig. 25). Detailed locations of groundwater-monitoring wells and associated water-quality conditions are provided in Anderholm (1987, pl. 4). The first region of elevated specific conductance and chloride is located in the northern part of the basin between San Acacia and Polvadera, New Mexico. Chloride concentrations approach 4,020 mg/L in this northernmost region. Elevated chloride concentrations in this part of the basin are likely from upward-flowing groundwater with elevated concentrations of dissolved solids derived from the distal end of the Albuquerque Basin (Anderholm, 1987; Wilkins, 1998; Mills, 2003; Hogan and others, 2007). The second region Anderholm (1987, pl. 4) identified as having elevated chloride is located in an area that extends from approximately 5 mi north and south of San Antonio, New Mexico. Chloride concentrations in this region are as high as 1,100 mg/L and most likely are from upward-flowing groundwater with elevated concentrations of dissolved solids or geothermal water that is leaking upward along the Capitan lineament (Anderholm, 1987). Results of seepage investigations performed by Newton and others (2002) during 2000–2002 indicate that the Rio Grande between San Acacia and San Marcial primarily is a losing reach (loss of Rio Grande water to the shallow alluvial aquifer; Appendix 3). However, during periods of elevated flow in the Rio Grande, Newton and others (2002) found that groundwater inflow to the Rio Grande occurs between Escondida and Highway 380 (Appendix 3). These seepage investigations coupled with the location of elevated dissolved solids identified by Anderholm, (1987) may provide information on where elevated dissolved solids enter the Rio Grande; however, additional hydrogeologic studies are needed to identify flow paths and underlying geologic structure that controls the flow of these dissolved solids to the Rio Grande and influence the potential for mitigation.

Another area with large concentrations of dissolved solids and chloride is the Luis Lopez Drain A (Mills, 2003). The Luis Lopez Drain A, which drains agricultural fields exclusively, is 9-km long and ultimately flows into the Socorro Drain (Mills, 2003). The dissolved-solids concentration was found to be 1,200 mg/L year round. The measured chloride concentration in the Luis Lopez A Drain was 232 mg/L, and the chloride-bromide ratio was 839. Mills (2003) argued that with no salt source evident at the surface, high chloride-bromide ratios, and historically consistent concentration of dissolved solids, it is probable that this drain intercepts upward-flowings saline groundwater.

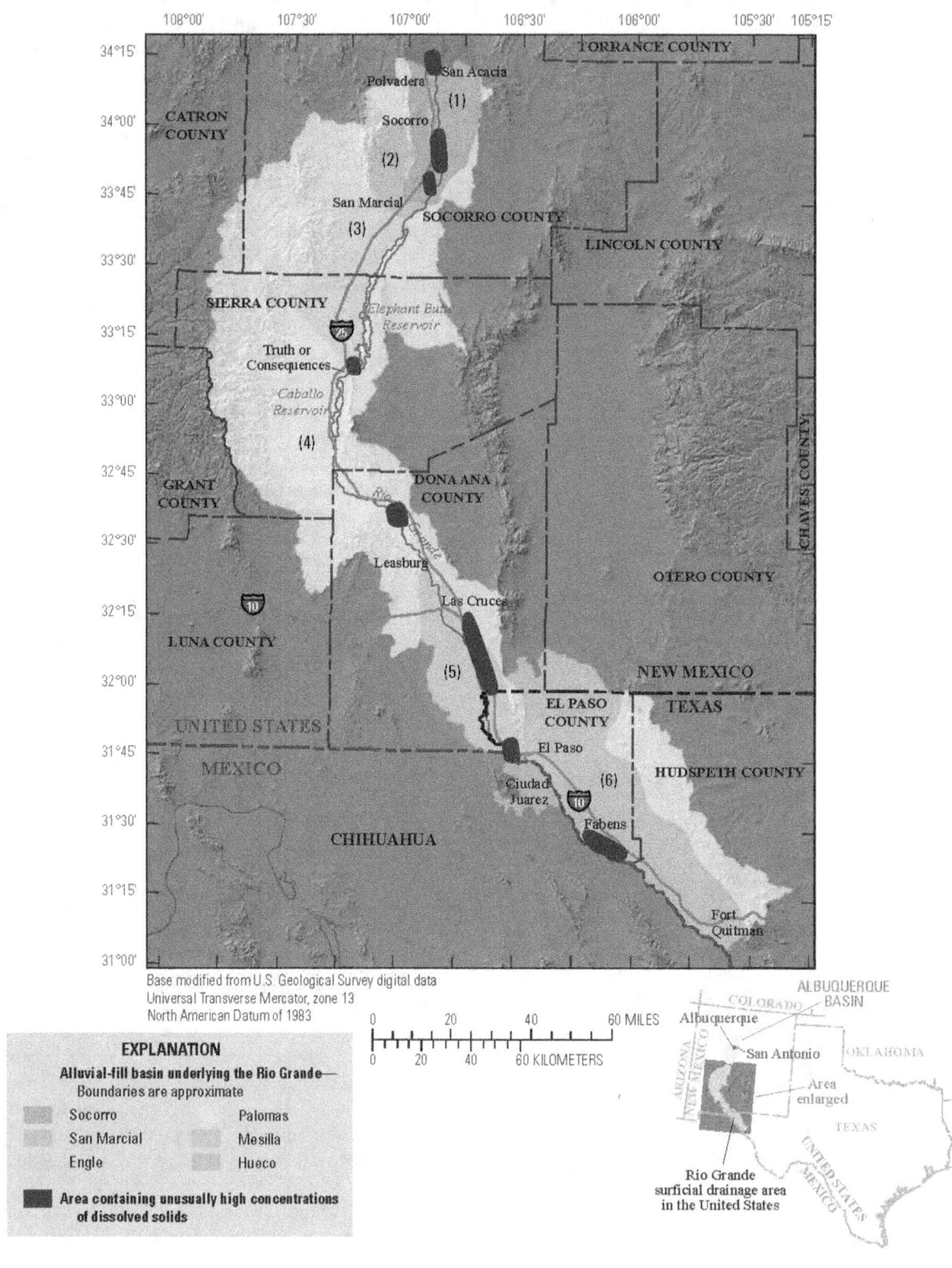

Figure 25.   The Rio Grande study area (white area) and the approximate location of areas containing unusually high concentrations of dissolved solids (in shaded black polygons) within each of the six alluvial-fill basins underlying the Rio Grande: (1) Socorro, (2) San Marcial, (3) Engle, (4) Palomas, (5) Mesilla, and (6) Hueco Basins. Boundaries of the six alluvial-fill basins are approximated from Wilkins (1986).

San Marcial Basin

The San Marcial Basin is the next basin south of the Socorro Basin. The Rio Grande flows southwest through the San Marcial Basin from San Marcial, New Mexico, to the upstream end of Elephant Butte Reservoir (Wilkins, 1986). Virtually no published information is available regarding the hydrogeology (Wilkins, 1986) and associated water quality of the San Marcial Basin.

Engle Basin

The Engle Basin is the next downstream alluvial-fill basin that underlies the Rio Grande (Wilkins, 1986). The Rio Grande flows through the Engle Basin from the upstream end of Elephant Butte Reservoir to just south of Truth or Consequences, New Mexico. The groundwater conditions in the Engle Basin were evaluated by Cox and Reeder (1962), who found that an area of thermal artesian groundwater, from the Magdalena group of Pennsylvanian and Permian age, discharges to the Rio Grande at Truth or Consequences, New Mexico. The thermal artesian groundwater, based on samples collected from well 14.4.4.211, has a sulfate concentration of 96 mg/L, a chloride concentration of 1,300-1,400 mg/L, a specific conductance of 4,450 microsiemens per centimeter (μS/cm), and a temperature of 104 °F (Cox and Reeder, 1962). Cox and Reeder (1962) delineate the area of thermal groundwater as water in wells and springs in the S1/2 sec. 33, T. 13 S., R. 4 W., and the N1/2 sec. 4, T. 14 S., R. 4W., within the limits of the town of Truth or Consequences north of the ridge of Precambrian rocks upon which Carrie Tingley Hospital is located (fig. 25). Based on two seepage investigations, performed November 30, 1960, and January 20, 1961, Cox and Reeder (1962) concluded that discharge increased by approximately 25 ft³/s (1.1 ft³/s /mile) from below Elephant Butte Dam to the upstream end of Caballo Reservoir (Appendix 3). Coupled water-quality data and seepage results indicate that the inflow of saline groundwater of geothermal origin occurs between Truth or Consequences and Williamsburg (located about 3 miles downstream from Truth or Consequences) (Cox and Reeder, 1962).

Processes governing the transport and storage of dissolved solids in Elephant Butte Reservoir are not completely understood. In a recent study, Lacey (2006) developed a model to simulate the water and chloride mass balance in Elephant Butte Reservoir. During this investigation, Lacey (2006) found strong evidence that suggests saline groundwater is discharging to Elephant Butte Reservoir and subsequently transported downstream. Lacey (2006) suggests that the discharge of saline groundwater into Elephant Butte Reservoir is minimized when the reservoir storage is high, such as during the 1979–93 period; conversely, the discharge of saline groundwater increases during periods when storage in Elephant Butte Reservoir is substantially reduced, such as during 1993–2004. Additional information is needed to better identify and quantify the processes that govern the transport and storage of dissolved solids into and out of Elephant Butte Reservoir.

Palomas Basin

The Palomas Basin is the next downstream basin from the Engle Basin that underlies the Rio Grande (Wilkins, 1986). The Rio Grande flows southeast through the Palomas Basin from just south of Truth or Consequences, New Mexico, to Selden Canyon north of Leasburg (Wilkins, 1986; Anderholm, 2002). The surface-water quality, quality of the groundwater in the shallow alluvial aquifer, and factors affecting water quality in the Palomas Basin were investigated and described by Anderholm (2002). Anderholm (2002) found that the concentrations of dissolved solids in the Rio Grande, agricultural drains, and groundwater in the shallow alluvial aquifer increased toward the southern end of the basin. The concentrations of dissolved solids in agricultural drains were always higher than the concentration of dissolved solids in the Rio Grande. Dissolved-solids concentrations double along the length of both the Hatch and Rincon Drains. Dissolved-solids concentrations in the Hatch Drain increased from approximately 650 mg/L to approximately 1,000 mg/L over a distance of 9 mi. Dissolved-solids concentrations in the Rincon Drain increased from approximately 800 mg/L to approximately 1,300 mg/L over a distance of 6 mi. The largest concentrations of dissolved solids were measured in groundwater wells completed in the shallow alluvial aquifer (well numbers 25, 26, 27, and 29) between the town of Rincon, New Mexico, and the discharge point of the Rincon Drain (fig. 25). Dissolved-solids concentrations in these groundwater wells ranged from 1,350 to 3,630 mg/L (Anderholm, 2002). Anderholm (2002) attributed the high concentrations of dissolved solids in the southern section of the Hatch and Rincon Drains and in the groundwater in the shallow alluvial aquifer near the distal end of the basin to inflow of regional groundwater. A major pathway for the movement of regional groundwater has been identified as groundwater transported from the Jornada del Muerto Basin eastward into the Palomas Basin (King and others, 1971). Results from seepage investigations show that groundwater inflow dominates the reach of the Rio Grande from below Caballo Dam to above Leasburg Dam (Appendix 3; Anderholm, 2002). Groundwater enters the Rio Grande for 24 mi below Caballo Dam and between the Hatch and Rincon Drains. Anderholm (2002) also showed that Rincon Drain intercepts considerable inflow of regional groundwater.

Mesilla Basin

The Mesilla Basin is the next downstream alluvial-fill basin from the Palomas Basin (Wilkins, 1968). The Rio Grande enters the Mesilla Basin as it flows through Selden Canyon at Leasburg, New Mexico, and continues flowing southeast to a narrow section of alluvial fill formed by the near-surface bedrock at El Paso, Texas. The water resources of the Mesilla Basin have been extensively studied for the past century. Detailed descriptions of the groundwater chemistry and the factors affecting groundwater chemistry are provided by Frenzel and others (1992) and Witcher and others (2004). Dissolved solids in the Mesilla Basin portion of the Rio Grande are controlled primarily by inflow of geothermal groundwater along the eastern portion of the Mesilla Basin and inflow of saline groundwater at the distal end of the Mesilla Basin (Frenzel and others, 1992; Witcher and others, 2004; Moore and other, 2008).

The inflow of geothermal groundwater has been identified as a major contributing source of dissolved solids in the Mesilla Basin portion of the Rio Grande (Frenzel and others, 1992; Witcher and others, 2004). Frenzel and others (1992, pl. 2) showed that the inflow of geothermal groundwater is not confined to a small area; rather, geothermal inflow of groundwater occurs along faults that underlie much of the eastern side of the Mesilla Basin (fig. 25). Frenzel and others (1992) identified two groundwater wells, 25S.3E.6.212 and 23S.2E.25.321, that characterize the chemistry of the geothermal groundwater. Another area of inflow of geothermal groundwater occurs southeast of the I–10 and I–25 interchange at Las Cruces, New Mexico (Witcher and others, 2004). Additionally, the East Drain, which runs along the eastern side of the Mesilla Basin from Anthony to Mesquite, is believed to intercept inflowing geothermal groundwater (Conover, 1954; Frenzel and others, 1992).

Inflow of saline groundwater also has been identified as a major contributing source of dissolved solids in the Mesilla Basin portion of the Rio Grande (Mills, 2003; Hogan and others, 2007; Moore and others, 2008). Most of the saline groundwater, termed brines in several of the references, flow upward at the distal end of the Mesilla Basin (fig. 25). It is in this area where the underlying geology forces saline groundwater at depth towards the surface and Rio Grande. Water chemistry in groundwater wells along the southern end of the Montoya Drain and above the narrow section at El Paso is indicative of upward-flowing saline groundwater. Concentrations of dissolved solids (4,010 mg/L), chloride (1,320 mg/L), sulfate (1,150 mg/L), and sodium plus potassium (1,310 mg/L) are elevated in well number JL-49-12-106 (Frenzel and others, 1992, pl. 5), located along the Montoya Drain north of the city limits of El Paso. Further south along the Montoya Drain, well number 29S.4E.6.243 (Frenzel and others, 1992, pl. 5) has even higher concentrations of chloride (4,000 mg/L), sulfate (3,600 mg/L), and sodium plus potassium (3,622 mg/L). In addition, the New Mexico Interstate Stream Commission and New Mexico Environment Department operate a monitoring-well network in the southern Palomas and Mesilla Basins. Results from quarterly monitoring of the groundwater network, during 2006–7, indicated that elevated dissolved solids and associated constituents extend from Santa Teresa, New Mexico (wells ISC-6 and ISC-7), to the region just

southeast of the confluence of the Montoya Drain and the Rio Grande (wells ISC-4, ISC-5 and El Paso Electric wells EPE-9, EPE-17, EPE-20, EPE-21; Daniel B. Stephens & Associates, Inc., 2008). Concentrations of dissolved solids (30,000 mg/L), chloride (18,000 mg/L), sulfate (6,200 mg/L), and sodium (7,700 mg/L; Moore and others, 2008) are elevated in groundwater well ISC-4 near the confluence of the Montoya Drain and the Rio Grande. Groundwater in the ISC-4 well commonly is used to represent the water chemistry of the upward-flowing saline groundwater (Mills, 2003; Moore and others, 2008; Bastien, 2009).

Seepage investigations have been conducted annually (1988–2008) by the USGS along a 62.4-mi reach of the Rio Grande that extends from below Leasburg Dam to El Paso (Courchesne Bridge) (http://nm.water.usgs.gov/projects/mesilla/). Results from these seepage investigations show that considerable gains to the Rio Grande (groundwater inflow) occur (1) from below Leasburg Dam to Shalem Bridge and (2) from Sunland Park Bridge to Courchesne Bridge (Appendix 3). Conversely, these seepage investigations also show that considerable losses occur (1) from Shalem Bridge to below Mesilla Dam and (2) from Vinton Bridge to Sunland Park Bridge.

The Montoya Drain drains a large area in the Mesilla Basin and has the largest flow and dissolved-solids load contribution to the Rio Grande of any other drains. The Montoya Drain accounts for more than half of the streamflow and dissolved-solids loads that are measured in the Rio Grande at El Paso (approximately 0.25 mi downstream from the Montoya Drain) during the nonirrigation season (Edward Nickerson, U.S. Geological Survey, written commun., June 16, 2009). The Montoya Drain generally carries water with values of specific conductance that range from 3,000 to 4,000 µS/cm and chloride concentrations that range from 500 to 675 mg/L. Geochemical and isotopic investigations reveal that the water chemistry of the Montoya Drain is derived from a mix of saline groundwater from geothermal and nongeothermal origins and Rio Grande water (Moore and others, 2008; Bastien, 2009). Therefore, salinity-mitigation efforts that reduce the mass of dissolved solids in inflowing saline groundwater should result in improvement of the quality of water delivered by the Montoya Drain and other irrigation drains.

Hueco Basin

The Hueco Basin is located southeast of the Mesilla Basin. The Rio Grande enters the Hueco Basin at the narrow section at El Paso and flows southeast to Fort Quitman, Texas (Wilkins, 1986). Extensive research in the Hueco Basin has focused on characterizing the various aquifer systems and associated hydrogeology (Hibbs, 1999; Hibbs and others, 2003; Anderholm and Heywood, 2003; Druhan and others, 2007). According to Hibbs and Merino (2007), the dominant source of dissolved solids in the Rio Grande within the Hueco Basin is the dissolution and subsequent transport of buried evaporites. However, Hibbs and Merino (2007) warned that the continued use of groundwater with elevated concentrations of dissolved solids for irrigation purposes will lead to continued degradation of soil conditions. Hibbs and Merino (2007) identified artesian groundwater flow and subsequent dissolution of evaporites associated with "paleo-phreatic playa beds" in a region approximately 2 mi southeast of Fabens, Texas (fig. 25). Within this area, Hibbs and Merino (2007) found chloride concentrations of 15,000 mg/L and chloride-bromide ratios of 5,800 in groundwater from the alluvial aquifer from approximately 150 to 250 ft below the land surface. Dissolved solids derived from the dissolution of the evaporates in the buried playa beds and subsequent transport by upwelling artesian groundwater are intercepted by agricultural drains and subsequently transported to the Rio Grande at various locations (Hibbs and Merino, 2007).

Municipal wastewater effluent from the Cities of El Paso and Fabens results in substantial dissolved-solids load to the Rio Grande in the Hueco Basin and needs to be evaluated. Miyamoto and others (1995) estimated that the average annual discharge of dissolved solids from the El Paso wastewater-treatment facility was 42,000 tons (approximately 10 percent of the load in the Rio Grande at El Paso) for the 1969–89 time period. Also, Mills (2003) showed that contributions from the Ascarate and Fabens waste channels deliver substantial amounts of chloride to the Rio Grande. Effluent from the wastewater-treatment facility in Fabens, Texas, discharges directly to the Fabens waste channel.

Future Studies and Monitoring Data

Looking forward, multiple water-resource managers from State and local agencies in New Mexico and Texas as well as many Federal agencies have united to form the Rio Grande Salinity Management Coalition (http://www.nmenv.state.nm.us/swqb/LowerRioGrande/). The unifying goal for the Coalition is to reduce the amount of dissolved solids that are transported and stored in the Rio Grande study area, thus ensuring that the Rio Grande water resources are of the quality that promotes the integrity and vitality of the agricultural, municipal, and ecological communities that rely on this limited resource. The following section provides recommendations for data-collection efforts and development of tools that could assist the Coalition in planning for, implementing, and evaluating mitigation efforts for dissolved solids in the Rio Grande. These recommendations are grouped into three categories: (1) monitoring of dissolved solids, (2) focused hydrogeology studies at inflow sources, and (3) modeling of dissolved solids.

Monitoring of Dissolved Solids

The collection of water samples to measure the concentration of dissolved solids and associated constituents from the Rio Grande, irrigation and agricultural-drain network, and underlying groundwater system is imperative for water-resource managers to effectively manage the surface-water and groundwater resources of the Rio Grande study area. Collection of these data provide a foundation for (1) improving the current understanding of dissolved-solids transport in the Rio Grande study area; (2) establishing water-quality goals; (3) building tools for water-resource managers to more effectively manage water-quality conditions; and (4) assessing changes in water-quality conditions in the Rio Grande resulting from salinity-mitigation efforts.

Rio Grande and Agricultural Drain Monitoring

The primary data-collection effort recommendation is to reestablish and(or) maintain monitoring of streamflow and water-quality conditions along the Rio Grande and major agricultural drains. Streamflow and water-quality monitoring data will be essential for the computation of dissolved-solids loads and the evaluation of long-term trends. The availability of annual load data is essential for determining the total amount of dissolved solids and associated water-quality constituents that are being transported or stored annually in the Rio Grande study area. These monitoring data also will allow for the evaluation of short- and long-term trends in water-quality conditions in the Rio Grande as a result of various dissolved-solids mitigation efforts. The computation of annual loads and evaluation of short- and long-term trends will provide water-resource managers with information regarding the influence dissolved-solids mitigation efforts are having on water-quality conditions.

Streamflow and water-quality conditions need to be monitored along the Rio Grande and at the distal end of major agricultural drains. The Rio Grande monitoring stations should include (1) San Acacia, (2) San Marcial, (3) below Elephant Butte Dam, (4) below Caballo Dam, (5) above Leasburg Dam, (6) at El Paso (Courchesne Bridge), (7) at Fabens (El Paso-Hudspeth County line), and (8) Fort Quitman. The irrigation-drain monitoring stations should include (1) Socorro Drain, (2) Rincon Drain, (3) Montoya Drain, and (4) Fabens waste canal. Water-quality data need to be collected monthly from the above listed locations. Water-quality samples need to be analyzed for dissolved solids, major ions (chloride, sulfate, carbonate, bicarbonate, sodium, calcium, and magnesium), bromide, and selected isotopes (used by Phillips and others, 2003; Hogan and others, 2007; Moore and others, 2008). Streamflow conditions need to be monitored continuously, such as 15-minute intervals, at each of the above locations; this monitoring will facilitate the computation of loads and evaluation of trends. A quality-assurance and quality-control plan needs to be developed and implemented to ensure that collected streamflow and water-quality data are of similar quality and are comparable among various collecting agencies and monitoring stations and over time.

The computation of water-quality constituent loads needs to be calculated and reported annually and employ a multiple linear-regression technique similar to the one used by Moore and Anderholm (2002). Examples of water-quality monitoring programs that incorporate multiple linear-regression analyses to compute loads and evaluate short- and long-term trends can be found for the Chesapeake Bay watershed (Langland and others, 2006) and the Mississippi River watershed (Aulenbach and others, 2007).

Groundwater/Surface-Water Interaction Investigation

Groundwater-seepage investigations are a commonly used approach to determine if a specified reach of river is receiving groundwater discharge or is losing surface water to the underlying alluvial aquifer (Harvey and Wagner, 2000; Rosenberry and LaBaugh, 2008). These investigations require the measurement of surface-water flow at the upstream and downstream locations of a specified reach and accounting for major surface inflows to and outflows from the reach. Differences in surface-water flow between two locations indicate whether groundwater (or other sources) is discharging to the surface-water system (gaining reach) or if surface water is being lost to the underlying alluvial aquifer (losing reach). The USGS has been performing fine-scale seepage investigations in the Rio Grande and contributing irrigation drains in the Mesilla Basin annually since 1988 (http://nm.water.usgs.gov/projects/mesilla/). These seepage investigations are performed during the nonirrigation period in order to maximize the groundwater-discharge signal. Results from seepage investigations in the Mesilla Basin have identified the reaches of the Rio Grande in the Mesilla Basin that are "gaining" and "losing." Additionally, the USGS quantifies the load of dissolved solids and associated constituents being gained or lost from each reach by collecting water-quality data in conjunction with each discharge measurement.

Therefore, the implementation of groundwater-seepage investigations is recommended for the reaches of the Rio Grande that drain the Socorro, San Marcial, Engle, Palomas, and Hueco Basins with continued support of the seepage investigation in the Mesilla Basin. These seepage investigations need to be executed during both the high-flow (irrigation season) and low-flow (nonirrigation season) periods. Seepage investigations during low-flow conditions best identify groundwater discharge to the surface-water system. Seepage investigations also need to be performed during high-flow conditions to quantify the volume of water and dissolved solids that are transported from the surface-water system and subsequently stored in the alluvial aquifer. Water-quality samples also need to be collected and analyzed for dissolved solids, major ions (chloride, sulfate, carbonate, bicarbonate, sodium, calcium, and magnesium), bromide, and selected isotopes (used by Phillips and others, 2003; Hogan and others, 2007; Moore and others, 2008). By including the collection of water-quality data during seepage investigations,

the flux of dissolved solids entering and leaving the Rio Grande can be calculated.

Groundwater Monitoring

The results from the mass-balance analysis performed by Williams (2001) and Witcher and others (2004) indicate that substantial amounts of dissolved solids are being stored in the Mesilla and Hueco Basins. One mechanism that has been attributed to the loss of surface water and associated dissolved solids from the Rio Grande is groundwater pumping for agricultural and municipal purposes (West, 1995; Hibbs and Boghici, 1999). The concern is that groundwater pumping will facilitate the degradation of groundwater quality in the Mesilla and Hueco Basins by (1) transporting water with high concentrations of dissolved solids from the Rio Grande into the upper levels of the alluvial aquifer, and (2) mixing water having high concentrations of dissolved solids in the upper zone of the alluvial aquifer with water at great depths containing low concentrations of dissolved solids (Walton and others, 1999). Therefore, it is recommended that a groundwater-monitoring network be instrumented that allows for (1) monitoring of current water-quality conditions, (2) evaluation of temporal and spatial changes in water-quality conditions, and (3) the potential for forecasting future water-quality conditions based on changes in municipal and agricultural water demands within the Mesilla and Hueco Basins.

Focused Hydrogeology Studies at Inflow Sources

Recent studies have determined that the dominant sources controlling dissolved solids in the Rio Grande study area are derived from the inflow of two saline groundwater sources – groundwater with elevated concentrations of dissolved solids and geothermal groundwater (Phillips and others, 2003; Hibbs and Merino, 2007; Hogan and others, 2007; Moore and others, 2008). As a result, focused hydrogeologic investigations are needed to (1) better define the spatial extent where elevated dissolved-solids concentrations have been identified, (2) identify locations and associated flow paths where dissolved solids and associated constituents are being discharged from the underlying alluvial aquifer to the Rio Grande, and (3) identify the influence that the underlying geology has on the transport of dissolved solids and potential for successful mitigation.

Helicopter Electromagnetic-Resistivity Data

The USGS, in Austin, Texas, in cooperation with the U.S. Bureau of Reclamation, has collected helicopter electromagnetic resistivity (HEM) data along parts of the Rio Grande and Rio Grande study area. These HEM data provide a measure of the electrical resistivity of the underlying alluvial aquifer (Rosenberry and LaBaugh, 2008). Changes in resistivity of the underlying alluvial aquifer can be related to changes in the properties of the alluvium (for example, gravel or clay) or changes in water-quality conditions (for example, high concentrations of dissolved solids or low concentrations of dissolved solids). The resistivity data are related ("ground-truthed") to measured subsurface properties and(or) water-quality conditions to obtain a three-dimensional framework for the specified property. Preliminary three-dimensional images for dissolved solids in the alluvial aquifer underlying the Rio Grande within the city limits of El Paso are now available (fig. 26). These images effectively identify the spatial extent of areas containing high concentrations of dissolved solids. HEM data for the distal end of the Mesilla Basin indicate that high-conductivity water with high concentrations of dissolved solids is in close proximity to the land surface in the area of the narrow section at El Paso (fig. 26). The spatial extent of these data is from levee to levee and reaches a depth of approximately 100 ft beneath the land surface.

HEM data need to be collected and processed for areas that currently are not covered by the work being performed by the USGS and U.S. Bureau of Reclamation. These HEM data could serve as a valuable tool for managing dissolved solids along the Rio Grande. By having a three-dimensional image of the spatial extent of dissolved solids in the alluvial aquifer, water-resource managers working with engineers and hydrologists, would be able to better identify areas of the Rio Grande where inflow of saline groundwater occurs. Additionally, HEM data could provide valuable information on the hydrogeologic framework for each of the alluvial-fill basins. This framework then could be incorporated into the groundwater model for each basin.

Hydrogeological and Tectonic Characterization at Inflow-Source Regions

Considerable research has been performed on the characterization of the hydrogeological matrix of the Rio Grande study area and associated alluvial basin (Chapin, 1971; Hawley, 1978; Riecker, 1979; Hawley and Kennedy, 2004; Hawley and others, 2005). The spatial scale associated with these hydrogeological characterizations has been focused primarily on the basin scale (for example, Mesilla Basin and Tularosa-Hueco Basin). These investigations have provided valuable information that describes the structure of the underlying geology and physical properties and processes that govern the transport of water through the associated alluvial aquifer. However, these investigations do not provide information, primarily because of scale, pertaining to the geological structure and transport processes that are specific to the delivery of saline groundwater to the Rio Grande. Hydrogeological and tectonic characterizations are needed in each of the identified source areas containing high concentrations of dissolved solids and associated constituents. It is likely that saline groundwater from geothermal and sedimentary sources are being transported into the shallow alluvial aquifer and Rio Grande along structural features, principally faults. A detailed investigation of the geological structures in the areas of the saline water introduction would contribute significantly to any assessment of the feasibility of active salinity mitigation.

Model Development for Dissolved-Solids Transport in the Rio Grande

Models are needed to simulate the transport and storage of dissolved solids in the Rio Grande and associated stream and irrigation network. These models would provide a tool for water-resource managers and researchers to (1) simulate and test the current conceptual model for the transport and storage of dissolved solids; (2) identify critical data and knowledge gaps that need to be filled in order to calibrate and improve the accuracy of the model to better understand solute transport in the Rio Grande; (3) evaluate the effect that variations in climate, land and water use, and water operations have on water quality in the Rio Grande; (4) develop a detailed budget for the transport and storage of dissolved solids and associated constituents; and (5) test the anticipated results of proposed salinity-mitigation projects. The models put in place to simulate dissolved solids in the Rio Grande study area ultimately will need to account for the role that surface water, groundwater, surface-water and groundwater interactions, water-management operations, irrigation, and groundwater withdrawals have in the transport and storage of dissolved solids. Several knowledge gaps exist within the current understanding of the transport and storage of dissolved solids in the Rio Grande study that need to be addressed as part of the model(s) development. These gaps are provided in the recommendations listed below.

Fate and Transport of Dissolved Solids in Elephant Butte and Caballo Reservoirs

The processes that govern transport and storage of dissolved solids into and out of Elephant Butte and Caballo Reservoirs are not well understood. It is essential for water-resource managers to understand the influence that the physical structure and water operations of these reservoirs has on the downstream transport of dissolved solids. Lacey (2006) developed a model to simulate the water and chloride mass balance in Elephant Butte Reservoir; however, additional studies are needed to expand on this research. First, the annual delivery and associated variability of dissolved solids into Elephant Butte and Caballo Reservoirs need to be quantified. These sources include dissolved solids that are transported by the Rio Grande as well as the direct discharge of deep saline groundwater. Second, a complex budget for Elephant Butte and Caballo Reservoirs needs to be developed that represents the annual inflow, outflow, and storage of dissolved solids. This added information regarding the effect of Elephant Butte

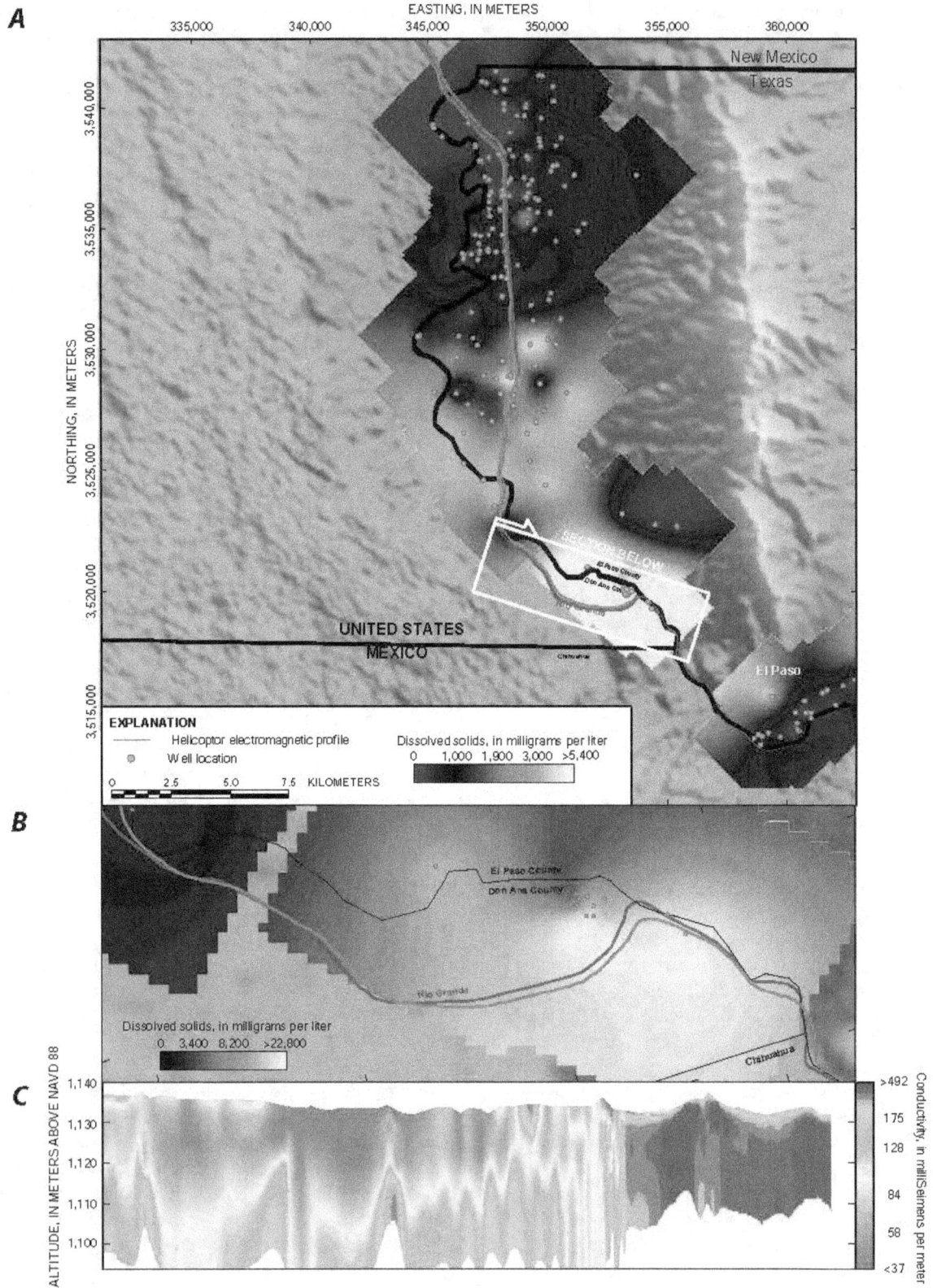

Figure 26. Images showing comparison of gridded dissolved solids (DS) measured from groundwater wells to gridded conductivity values measured from helicopter electromagnetic (HEM) data: (*A*) Map showing gridded DS at the study area and location of the HEM profile, (*B*) map showing gridded DS at the location of the HEM section, and (*C*) section showing gridded conductivity values from the HEM profile.

and Caballo Reservoirs on dissolved solids will be essential for (1) developing improved mass-balance budgets for downstream reaches of the Rio Grande and (2) constructing water-quality model(s) for the Rio Grande in the study area.

Improved Mass-Balance Budgets for Rio Grande Dissolved Solids

Continued improvement in the detail of the dissolved-solids mass-balance budgets is recommended. Bastien (2009) developed the latest mass-balance budget for reaches between San Acacia, New Mexico, and El Paso, Texas, in which the inflow of regional groundwater and the inflow of saline groundwater were the dominant sources of dissolved solids. Additionally, Bastien (2009) established that the difference between the estimated inflow and measured outflow of dissolved solids were a result of chemical reactions with various mineral phases (mineral dissolution and precipitation reactions). Building upon the detailed mass-balance budgets established by Bastien (2009), three core processes need to be further resolved and refined for each reach in the Rio Grande study area. These processes are (1) direct quantification of the load of dissolved solids and major ions associated with the inflow of saline groundwater (geothermal and nongeothermal); (2) further quantification of the flux of dissolved solids that are derived from the dissolution of minerals from the soils beneath agricultural and riparian areas; and (3) identification and quantification of processes that store dissolved solids in each reach, such as mineral precipitation, ion exchange, and groundwater pumping. A major challenge that will have to be addressed is quantifying the balance between processes that act as sources (groundwater inflow) and sinks (mineral precipitation and groundwater storage) for dissolved-solids transport in each reach. Information provided by the tools and data collection recommended above will help to improve the accuracy and level of detail in the mass-balance budgets. Finally, the complex mass-balance budgets developed by Bastien (2009) only represent reaches in the Rio Grande study area that extend from San Acacia, New Mexico, to El Paso, Texas. A complex mass-balance budget for dissolved solids and major ions (chloride, sulfate, bicarbonate, sodium, potassium, and magnesium) is needed for the reach of the Rio Grande that extends from El Paso, Texas, to Fort Quitman, Texas.

References Cited

Anderholm, S.K., 1987, Hydrogeology of the Socorro and La Jencia basins, Socorro County, New Mexico: U.S. Geological Survey Water-Resources Investigations Report 84–4342, 62 p.

Anderholm, S.K., 2002, Water-quality assessment of the Rio Grande Valley, Colorado, New Mexico, and Texas—Surface-water quality, shallow ground-water quality, and factors affecting water quality in the Rincon Valley, south-central New Mexico, 1994–95: U.S. Geological Survey Water-Resources Investigations Report 02–4188, 117 p.

Anderholm, S.K., and Heywood, C.E., 2003, Chemistry and age of ground water in the southwestern Hueco Bolson, New Mexico and Texas: U.S. Geological Survey Water-Resources Investigations Report 02–4237, 16 p.

Anning, D.W., Bauch, N.J., Gerner, S.J., Flynn, M.E., Hamlin, S.N., Moore, S.J., Schaefer, D.H., Anderholm, S.K., and Spangler, L.E., 2007, Dissolved solids in basin-fill aquifers and streams in the Southwestern United States: U.S. Geological Survey Scientific Investigations Report 2006–5315, 336 p.

Aulenbach, B.T., Buxton, H.T., Battaglin, W.A., and Coupe, R.H., 2007, Streamflow and nutrient fluxes of the Mississippi-Atchafalaya River Basin and subbasins for the period of record through 2005: U.S. Geological Survey Open-File Report 2007–1080, available only online at http://pubs.usgs.gov/of/2007/1080/.

Autobee, Robert, 1994, Rio Grande Project, accessed August 21, 2012 at http://www.usbr.gov/projects//ImageServer?imgName=Doc_1305577076373.pdf.

Bastien, E.M., 2009, Solute budget of the Rio Grande above El Paso, Texas: Socorro, N. Mex., New Mexico Institute of Mining and Technology, M.S. thesis, 232 p.

Booker, J.F., Michelsen, A.M., Ward, F.A., 2008, Economic impact of alternative policy responses to prolonged and severe drought in the Rio Grande Basin: Water Resources Research, v.41 W02026, doi:10.1029/2004WR003486.

Bothern, L.R., 2003, Geothermal salt intrusion into the Mesilla basin aquifers and the Rio Grande, Dona Ana County, New Mexico: Las Cruces, N. Mex., New Mexico State University, M.S. thesis, 127 p.

Bryan, Kirk, 1938, Geology and ground-water conditions of the Rio Grande depression in Colorado and New Mexico, in National Resources Committee, 1938, Regional planning report part VI, The Rio Grande joint investigation in the upper Rio Grande Basin in Colorado, New Mexico, and Texas,1936–1937: Washington, D.C., U.S. Government Printing Office, p. 197–225.

Chapin, C.E., 1971, The Rio Grande Rift – part 1—Modifications and additions, in James, H.L., ed., Guidebook of the San Luis Basin, Colorado: New Mexico Geological Society, 22nd Field Conference, p. 191–201.

Colorado River Basin Salinity Control Forum, 2008, 2008 review, water quality standards for salinity, Colorado River system: Colorado River Basin Salinity Control Forum, October 2008, accessed June 15, 2009, at http://www.coloradoriversalinity.org/docs/2008%20Review.pdf.

Conover, C.S., 1954, Ground-water conditions in the Rincon and Mesilla Valleys and adjacent areas in New Mexico: U.S. Geological Survey Water-Supply Paper 1230, 200 p.

Cox, E.R., and Reeder, H.O., 1962, Ground-water conditions in the Rio Grande valley between Truth or Consequences and Las Palomas, Sierra County, New Mexico: New Mexico State Engineer Technical Report 25, p. 45.

Daniel B. Stephens & Associates, Inc., 2008, Annual report for the lower Rio Grande water quality monitoring program, May 2006 through February 2007: Albuquerque and Los Alamos, N. Mex., Consulting report prepared for New Mexico Environment Department and New Mexico Interstate Stream Commission, June 30, 2008.

Druhan, J.L., Hogan, J.F., Eastoe, C.J., Hibbs, B.J., and Hutchison, W.R., 2007, Hydrogeologic controls on groundwater recharge and salinization: A geochemical analysis of the northern Hueco Bolson aquifer, Texas, USA: Hydrogeology Journal, v. 16, no. 2, p. 281–296.

Eastoe, C.J., Hibbs, B.J., Olivas, A.G., Hogan, J.F., Hawley, John, and Hutchison, W.R., 2007, Isotopes in the Hueco Bolson aquifer, Texas (USA) and Chihuahua (Mexico): Local and general implications for recharge sources in alluvial basins: Hydrogeology Journal, v. 16, no. 4, p. 737–747.

Ellis, S.R., Levings, G.W., Carter, L.F., Richey, S.F., and Radell, M.J., 1993, Rio Grande Valley, Colorado, New Mexico, and Texas: Journal of the American Water Resources Association, v. 29, no. 4, p. 617–648.

Frenzel, P.F., Kaehler, C.A., and Anderholm, S.K., 1992, Geohydrology and simulation of ground-water flow in the Mesilla Basin, Dona Ana County, New Mexico, and El Paso County, Texas, with a section on water quality and geochemistry: U.S. Geological Survey Professional Paper 1407–C, 105 p.

Harvey, J.W., and Wagner, B.J., 2000, Quantifying hydrologic interactions between streams and their subsurface hyporheic zones, in Jones, J.B., and Mulholland, P.J., eds., Streams and Ground Waters: San Diego, Calif., Academic Press, p. 3–44.

Hawley, J.W., 1978, Guidebook to the Rio Grande Rift in New Mexico and Colorado: New Mexico Bureau of Mines and Mineral Resources Circular 163, 241 p.

Hawley, J.W., and Kennedy, J.F., 2004, Creation of a digital hydrogeologic framework model of the Mesilla Basin and southern Jornada del Muerto Basin: Las Cruces, N. Mex., New Mexico Water Resources Research Institute of New Mexico State University, Technical Completion Report 332, 123 p.

Hawley, J.W., Kennedy, J.F., Ortiz, Marquita, and Carrasco, Sean, 2005, Digital hydrogeologic framework model of the Rincon Valley and adjacent areas of Dona Ana, Sierra and Luna Counties, NM: Las Cruces, N. Mex., New Mexico Water Resources Research Institute of New Mexico State University, addendum to Technical Completion Report 332, accessed October 22, 2009, at http://wrri.nmsu.edu/publish/techrpt/tr332/cdrom/addendum.pdf.

Helm, D., 1984, Analysis of sedimentary skeletal deformation in a confined aquifer and the resulting drawdown, in Rosenshein, J.S., and Bennett, G.D., eds., Groundwater Hydraulics: Washington, D.C., American Geophysical Union, Water Resources Monograph 9, p. 29–82.

Helsel, D.R., and Hirsch, R.M., 1992, Statistical methods in water resources: New York, N.Y., Elsevier, 529 p.

Hem, J.D., 1992, Study and interpretation of the chemical characteristics of natural water: U.S. Geological Survey Water-Supply Paper 2254, 263 p.

Heywood, C.E., and Yager, R.M., 2003, Simulated ground-water flow in the Hueco Bolson, an alluvial-basin aquifer system near El Paso, Texas: U.S. Geological Survey Water-Resources Investigations Report 02–4108, 73 p.

Hibbs, B.J., 1999, Hydrogeologic and water quality issues along the El Paso/Juarez Corridor: An international case: Environmental and Engineering Geoscience, v. 5, no. 1, p. 27–39.

Hibbs, B.J., and Boghici, R.N., 1999, On the Rio Grande aquifer: Flow relationships, salinization, and environmental problems from El Paso to Fort Quitman, Texas: Environmental and Engineering Geoscience, v. 5, p. 51–59.

Hibbs, B.J., and Merino, Mercedes, 2007, Discovering a geologic salinity source in the Rio Grande aquifer: Southwest Hydrology, July/August 2007, v. 6, no. 4, p. 20–23.

Hibbs, B.J., Phillips, F.M., Hogan, J.F., Eastoe, C.J., Hawley, J.W., Kennedy, J.F., Nunez, Francisco, Granados, Alfredo, and Kretzschmar, Thomas, 2003, Binational study of the surface and ground water resources of the El Paso/Juarez International Corridor: Universities Council on Water Resources, Water Resources Update Issue 125, June 2003, p. 25–30.

Hogan, J.F., Phillips, F.M., Mills, S.K., Hendrickx, J.M.H., Ruiz, Joaquin, Chesley, J.T., Asmerom, Yemane, 2007, Geologic origins of salinization in a semi-arid river: The role of sedimentary basin brines: Geology, v. 35, no. 12, p. 1063–1066.

Hutchison, W.R., 2006, Groundwater management in El Paso, Texas: El Paso, Tex., University of Texas, Ph.D. dissertation, 329 p.

Jackson, R.B., Carpenter, S.R., Dahm, C.N., McKnight, D.M., Naiman, R.J., Postel, S.L., and Running, S.W., 2001, Water in a changing world: Ecological Applications, v. 11, no. 4, p. 1027–1045.

Keller, G.R., and Baldridge, W.S., 1999, The Rio Grande Rift, a geological and geophysical overview: Rocky Mountain Geology, v. 34, no. 1, p. 121–130.

King, W.E., Hawley, J.W., Taylor, A.M., and Wilson, R.P., 1971, Geology and ground-water resources of central and western Dona Ana County, New Mexico: New Mexico Bureau of Mines and Mineral Resources Hydrologic Report 1, 64 p.

Lacey, H.F., 2006, Quantification and characterization of chloride sources in the Rio Grande: Socorro, N. Mex., New Mexico Institute of Mining and Technology, M.S. thesis, 166 p.

Langland, M.J., Raffensperger, J.P., Moyer, D.L., Landwehr, J.M., and Schwarz, G.E., 2006, Changes in streamflow and water quality in selected nontidal basins in the Chesapeake Bay watershed, 1985–2004: U.S. Geological Survey Scientific Investigations Report 2006–5178, 75 p.

Leggat, E.R., Lowry, M.E., and Hood, J.W., 1962, Ground-water resources of the lower Mesilla Valley, Texas and New Mexico: Texas Water Commission Bulletin 6203, 191 p.

Lippincott, J.B., 1939, Southwest border water problems: Journal of the American Water Works Association, v. 31, p. 1–28.

Longworth, J.W., Valdez, J.M., Magnuson, M.L., Albury, E.S., and Keller, Jerry, 2008, New Mexico water use by categories, 2005: New Mexico Office of the State Engineer Technical Report 52, 111 p.

Mills, S.K., 2003, Quantifying salinization of the Rio Grande using environmental tracers: Socorro, N. Mex., New Mexico Institute of Mining and Technology, M.S. thesis, 397 p.

Miyamoto, Seiichi, Fenn, L.B., and Swietlik, D., 1995, Flow, salts, and trace elements in the Rio Grande: A review: Texas Water Resources Institute Technical Report 169, 30 p.

Moore, S.J., and Anderholm, S.K., 2002, Spatial and temporal variations in streamflow, dissolved solids, nutrients, and suspended sediment in the Rio Grande Valley study unit, Colorado, New Mexico, and Texas, 1993–95: U.S. Geological Survey Water-Resources Investigations Report 02–4224, 52 p.

Moore, S.J., Basset, R.L., Liu, Beiling, Wolf, C.P., and Doremus, Dale, 2008, Geochemical tracers to evaluate hydrogeologic controls on river salinization: Ground Water, May–June 2008, p. 489–501.

Newton, B.T., 2005, Geologic controls on shallow groundwater in the Socorro Basin, New Mexico: Socorro, N. Mex., New Mexico Institute of Mining and Technology, M.S. thesis, 163 p.

Newton, B.T., Kuhn, S., Johnson, P., and Hathaway, D.L., 2002, Investigation of flow and seepage conditions on a critical reach of the Rio Grande, New Mexico, in Summer Specialty Conference on Ground Water/Surface Water Interactions, Keystone, Colo., July 1–3, 2002, Proceedings: Keystone, Colo., American Water Resources Association, p. 581–586.

National Resources Committee, 1938, Regional Planning Report VI, Rio Grande joint investigation in the upper Rio Grande basin in Colorado, New Mexico, and Texas, 1936–1937: Washington, D.C., U.S. Government Printing Office, 566 p.

Phillips, F.M., Hogan, J.F., Mills, S.K., and Hendrickx, J.M.H., 2003, Environmental tracers applied to quantifying causes of salinity in arid-region rivers: Results from the Rio Grande, southwestern USA, in Alsharhan, A.S., and Wood, W.W., eds., Water Resources Perspectives: Evaluation, Management and Policy: New York, Elsevier Science, p. 327–334.

Piper, A.M., 1944, A graphic procedure in the geochemical interpretation of water analyses: American Geophysical Union Transactions, v. 25, p. 914–923.

Plummer, L.N., Bexfield, L.M., Anderholm, S.K., Sanford, W.E., and Busenberg, Eurybiades, 2004, Geochemical characterization of ground-water flow in the Santa Fe group aquifer system, Middle Rio Grande Basin, New Mexico: U.S. Geological Survey Water-Resources Investigations Report 03–4131, 395 p.

Riecker, R.E., ed., 1979, Rio Grande Rift: Tectonics and magmatism: Washington, D.C., American Geophysical Union, 438 p.

Rister, M.E., Sturdivant, A.W., Lacewell, R.D., and Michelsen, A.M., 2011, Challenges and Opportunities for Water of the Rio Grande: Journal of Agricultural and Applied Economics, v. 43, p. 367–378.

Rosenberry, D.O., and LaBaugh, J.W., 2008, Field techniques for estimating water fluxes between surface water and ground water: U.S. Geological Survey Techniques and Methods 4–D2, 128 p.

Sanford, W.E., Plummer, L.N., McAda, D.P., Bexfield, L.M., and Anderholm, S.K., 2004, Hydrochemical tracers in the middle Rio Grande Basin, USA: 2. Calibration of a groundwater-flow model: Hydrogeology Journal, v. 12, p. 389–407.

Schmid, Wolfgang, Hanson, R.T., Maddock, Thomas, III, and Leake, S.A., 2006, User guide for the farm process (FMP1) for the U.S. Geological Survey's modular three-dimensional finite-difference ground-water flow model, MODFLOW–2000: U.S. Geological Survey Techniques and Methods 6–A17, 127 p.

Stabler, Herman, 1911, Some stream waters of the western United States: U.S. Geological Survey Water-Supply Paper 274, 188 p.

Texas Water Development Board, 2007, 2005 Texas water use summary estimates: Texas Water Development Board, accessed June 15, 2009, at http://www.twdb.state.tx.us/data/water_use/2005est/2005wus.htm.

Thorn, C.R., McAda, D.P., and Kernodle, J.M., 1993, Geohydrologic framework and hydrologic conditions in the Albuquerque Basin, central New Mexico: U.S. Geological Survey Water-Resources Investigations Report 93–44149, 106 p.

Walton, John, Ohlmacher, Gregory, Utz, Dennis, and Kutianawala, Murtaza, 1999, Response of the Rio Grande and shallow ground water in the Mesilla Bolson to irrigation, climate stress, and pumping: Environmental and Engineering Geoscience, v. 5, no. 1, p. 41–50.

West, Francis, 1995, The Mesilla Valley: A century of water resources investigations, in 40th Annual New Mexico Water Conference, Reaching the limits: Stretching the resources of the Lower Rio Grande, proceedings, October 1995: Las Cruces, N. Mex., New Mexico Water Resources Research Institute of New Mexico State University, p. 21–28.

Wilcox, L.V., 1957, Analysis of salt balance and salt-burden data on the Rio Grande, in Duisberg, P.C., ed., Problems of the Upper Rio Grande: An arid zone river: Socorro, N. Mex., U.S. Commission for Arid Improvement and Development Publication 1, p. 39–44.

Wilcox, L.V., 1968, Discharge and salt burden of the Rio Grande above Fort Quitman Texas, and salt-balance conditions on the Rio Grande project, Summary report for the 30-year period 1934–1963: U.S. Salinity Laboratory Research Report 113.

Wilkins, D.W., 1986, Geohydrology of the southwest alluvial basins regional aquifer-systems analysis, parts of Colorado, New Mexico, and Texas: U.S. Geological Survey Water-Resources Investigations Report 84–4224, 61 p.

Wilkins, D.W., 1998, Summary of the southwest alluvial basins regional aquifer-system analysis in parts of Colorado, New Mexico, and Texas: U.S. Geological Survey Professional Paper 1407–A, 49 p.

Williams, J.H., 2001, Salt balance in the Rio Grande project area from San Marcial, New Mexico, to Fort Quitman, Texas: Las Cruces, N. Mex., New Mexico State University, M.S. thesis, 42 p.

Wilson, C.A., White, R.R., Orr, B.R., and Roybal, R.G., 1981, Water resources of the Rincon and Mesilla Valleys and adjacent areas, New Mexico: New Mexico Office of the State Engineer Technical Report 43, 514 p.

Witcher, J.C., King, J.P., Hawley, J.W., Kennedy, J.F., Williams, J., Cleary, M., and Bothern, L.R., 2004, Sources of salinity in the Rio Grande and Mesilla Basin groundwater: Las Cruces, N. Mex., New Mexico Water Resources Research Institute of New Mexico State University, Technical Report 330, 168 p.

Yuan, Fasong, and Miyamoto, Seiichi, 2004, Influence of the Pacific decadal oscillation on hydrochemistry of the Rio Grande, USA, and Mexico: Geochemistry, Geophysics, Geosystems, v. 5, no. 12, p. 1–10.

Appendixes 1–3

Appendix 1. Average annual and seasonal streamflow and dissolved solids concentration, flow-weighted concentration and load for monitoring stations along the Rio Grande between San Marcial, New Mexico and Fort Quitman Texas.

[ft³/s, cubic feet per second; mg/L, milligrams per liter]

Rio Grande monitoring station	Average annual streamflow (ft³/s)[1]	Average monthly streamflow[2]		Average annual flow-weighted dissolved solids concentration (mg/L)[1]	Average annual dissolved solids concentration (mg/L)[1]
		Non-irrigation season (ft³/s)	Irrigation season (ft³/s)		
At San Marcial, NM	1,041	784	1,396	528	586
Below Elephant Butte, NM	960	372	1,390	516	512
Below Caballo, NM	947	158	1,101	545	612
Above Leasburg, NM	901	149	1,436	591	660
At El Paso, TX	597	201	848	746	1,053
At Fort Quitman, TX	198	192	210	2,069	3,275

Rio Grande monitoring station	Average dissolved solids concentration[2]		Average annual dissolved solids load (tons/day)[1]	Average dissolved solids load[2]	
	Non-irrigation season (mg/L)	Irrigation season (mg/L)		Non-irrigation season (tons/day)	Irrigation season (tons/day)
At San Marcial, NM	563	602	1,296	917	1,557
Below Elephant Butte, NM	533	497	1,259	546	1,805
Below Caballo, NM	711	592	1,319	216	1,476
Above Leasburg, NM	801	559	1,364	309	2,186
At El Paso, TX	1,464	763	1,168	567	1,569
At Fort Quitman, TX	3,355	3,219	916	1,127	1,119

[1]Data from Wilcox, 1968 (Dates represented 1934 through 1963).

[2]Data from Wilcox, 1968; Williams, 2001 (Dates represented 1934 through 1968 (Wilcox, 1968) and 1969 through 1999 sporadically (Williams, 2001).

Appendix 2.   Description of groundwater regions, in the Rio Grande study area, with unusually high concentration of dissolved solids and/or chloride.

[mg/L, milligrams per liter; DS, dissolved solids; Alb. Albuquerque; gw, groundwater; SC, specific conductance]

Basin	Location/ areal extent	Sample type	Chloride (mg/L)	DS (mg/L)	Probable source(s)	Data source
Socorro Basin	S. Albuquerque Basin and N. Socorro Basin between La Joya and Polvadera, NM	gw	270–4,020		Upward flow of gw brines from distal end of Alb. basin	Anderholm, 1987
	5 miles north and south of San Antonio, NM	gw	260–1,100		Upward flow of gw brines/geothermal gw along Capitan lineament	Anderholm, 1987
	Area 5.5 miles long near Luis Lopez Drain	gw	232	1,200	Upward flowing gw brines intercepted by drain	Mills, 2003
San Marcial Basin	No published information	gw				
Engle Basin	Elephant Butte Reservoir, NM	gw			Discharge of gw brines	Lacey, 2006
	Truth or Consequences, NM	gw	1,300; 1,400	SC = 4,450; TDS = 2,600	Geothermal gw from Magdalena group	Cox and Reeder, 1962; Moore and others, 2008
Palomas Basin	Hatch Drain 9 mile long reach near Hatch,NM	drain		650 to 1,000 along drain	Regional gw inflow from Joranada del Muerto Basin	Anderholm, 2002
	Rincon Drain 6 mile long reach near Rincon, NM	drain		800 to 1,300 along drain	Regional gw inflow from Joranada del Muerto Basin	Anderholm, 2002
	Alluvial wells in area from Rincon, NM to Rincon Drain discharge point	shallow gw		1,350 to 3,630	Regional gw inflow from Joranada del Muerto Basin	Anderholm, 2002
Mesilla Basin	Eastern Mesilla Basin (general)	gw	940		Inflow of geothermal gw along faults underlying eastern Mesilla Basin	Frenzel and Kaehler, 1992; Witcher and others, 2004
	Eastern Mesilla Basin - East Drain from Anthony, NM to Mesquite, NM	drain			Upward gw flow intercepted by drain	Frenzel and Kaehler, 1992
	Distal end of Mesilla Valley - near Montoya Drain and above El Paso, TX	gw well	4,000		Upward gw flow at distal end of basin	Frenzel and Kaehler, 1992
	Distal end of Mesilla Valley near Montoya drain and confluence with Rio Grande	gw well	18,000	30,000	Upward flow of gw brines at distal end of basin	Moore and others, 2008
	Distal end of Mesilla Valley - Montoya Drain	drain	640	2,400	Upward flow of gw brines at distal end of basin	Moore and others, 2008
Hueco Basin	Downstream of El Paso Wastewater Treatment Facility	effluent		1,390	Wastewater effluent	Miyamoto and others, 1995
	Ascarate & Fabens waste channel				Wastewater effluent	Mills, 2003
	Area 2 miles SE of Fabens, TX	gw	15,000		Artesian flow through evaporite deposits to the Rio Grande	Hibbs and Merino, 2007

Appendix 3.   Description of gains and losses in Rio Grande streamflow and flux of dissolved solids from inflowing groundwater for each reach of the Rio Grande.

[GW, groundwater; ft³/s/mile, cubic feet per second per mile; ~, approximately]

Reach	Basin	Source	Gains in Rio Grande streamflow from groundwater inflow	Losses in Rio Grande discharge to groundwater recharge	Flux of groundwater dissolved solids from seepage and brine inflow (Bastien, 2009, for 1980–89) tons per month
San Acacia to San Marcial	Socorro and San Marcial	Newton and others, 2002		From San Acacia to San Marcial during both Irrigation and nonirrigation periods	GW Seepage flux = 404; Brine flux = 3,839
San Acacia to San Marcial	Socorro and San Marcial	Newton and others, 2002	Between Escondida and North Bosque Hwy 380		
San Marcial to below Elephant Butte	Engle				GW seepage flux = 273; Brine flux = 129
Below Elephant Butte to Caballo Reservoir	Engle/ Palomas	Cox and Reeder, 1962	Between Williamsburg and Caballo Reservoir (~1.1 ft³/s/mile)		GW seepage flux = 1,011; Brine flux = 2,013
Below Caballo Reservoir to Above Leasburg	Palomas	Anderholm, 2002; Wilson and others, 1981	From Caballo to 24 miles downstream (1.5 ft³/s/mile)		
Below Caballo Reservoir to Above Leasburg	Palomas	Anderholm, 2002; Wilson and others, 1981	Between Hatch and Rincon Drains (0.3 ft³/s/mile)		
Below Caballo Reservoir to Above Leasburg	Palomas	Anderholm, 2002	Rincon Drain (~0.5 ft³/s/mile)		
Above Leasburg to El Paso	Mesilla	http://nm.water. usgs.gov/projects/ mesilla; Wilson and others, 1981	From below Leasburg dam to ~ 10 miles downstream near Shalem Bridge		
Above Leasburg to El Paso	Mesilla	http://nm.water. usgs.gov/projects/ mesilla; Wilson and others, 1981		From Shalem Bridge (12.5 miles) to Below Mesilla Dam	
Above Leasburg to El Paso	Mesilla	http://nm.water. usgs.gov/projects/ mesilla; Wilson and others, 1981		From Vinton Bridge (14 miles) to Sunland Park Bridge	
Above Leasburg to El Paso	Mesilla	http://nm.water. usgs.gov/projects/ mesilla	From Sunland Park Bridge to Courchesne Bridge		
Bbelow Caballo Reservoir to El Paso	Palomas/Mesilla	Bastien, 2009			GW seepage flux = 5,320; Brine flux = 3,687
El Paso to Fort Quitman	Hueco	http://www.ibwc. state.gov/Water_ Data/binational_ waters.htm	From El Paso/ Hudspeth County Line to Fort Quitman